Project Scope

How To Scale Your AI Law Firm
Impact of AI In Legal Industry

How Artificial Intelligence is Adding Value, Amplifying Expertise, and Transforming Careers

1st Edition

By

Hamid Kohan

DEDICATION

To my dear family,

This book is dedicated to you with all my love and gratitude. You have been my constant source of support and inspiration throughout my journey in legal industry, and I could not have accomplished any of my achievements without your unwavering love and encouragement.

To my wife Nazi, you have been my rock and my partner in every sense of the word.

To my boys Bobby, Shayan, Jaden, and Arya, you have brought me so much joy and purpose, and I am proud of the young men, you are becoming. Your boundless energy, curiosity, and compassion for others inspire me every day.

As I navigate the complex and challenging world of law, your love and support have given me the strength to persevere and to fight for justice.

Thank you for being my greatest blessings, my greatest joys, and my greatest reasons for living. I dedicate this book to you with all my heart.

Love,

Hamid Kohan

Copyright © 2023

All Rights Reserved

CONTENTS

Dedication	ii
Acknowledgment	vi
Introduction	vi
Chapter 1: Your Law Firm and AI	1
Chapter 2: AI in the intake process	25
Chapter 3: AI in operation	37
Chapter 4: AI in Marketing	50
Chapter 5: AI in Case Litigation	65
Chapter 6: AI in Law Practice Process Automation	79
Chapter 7: AI in Finance	90
Chapter 8: AI and Different Practices	103
AI Resources List	116
About Author	143

ACKNOWLEDGMENT

To my amazing wife Nazy,

You have been my rock and my partner in every sense of the word.

This book is dedicated to you, recognizing your unwavering support and love for our family. Your role as a remarkable mother to our sons has been invaluable, and I am truly grateful for the positive impact you've made on their lives.

I appreciate the unwavering encouragement you've given me throughout my professional career over the last 25 years.

INTRODUCTION

Artificial Intelligence (AI) has become an integral part of our lives. The concept of machines that can think, learn and perform tasks autonomously is no longer a distant dream but a reality. In this article, we will delve into the history of AI and why people began investing in it. We will also discuss the different types of AI and their integration in various fields, and finally, we will talk about the inevitability of AI being the next technological step.

The history of AI can be traced back to the 1950s when scientists first began exploring the concept of machines that could perform tasks that would typically require human intelligence. The first AI program was developed in 1951 by Christopher Strachey, a British computer scientist, who wrote a checkers-playing program. The term "Artificial Intelligence" was coined in 1956 by John McCarthy, a computer scientist, and his colleagues during the Dartmouth Conference, which marked the beginning of AI research.

The early years of AI were slow due to limited computing power and the lack of sophisticated algorithms. However, with technological advancements, AI started gaining traction in the 1980s and 1990s. Machine learning techniques enabled computers to learn from data and improve their performance.

The types of AI can be categorized into ANI (Artificial Narrow Intelligence), AGI (Artificial General Intelligence), and ASI (Artificial Super Intelligence). ANI is the most commonly used form of AI designed to perform specific tasks within a limited domain. This includes tasks like image recognition, language translation, and recommendation systems. AGI is designed to have human-like intelligence, enabling machines to learn and adapt to new situations and perform various tasks like humans. ASI is a theoretical form of AI that can perform any intellectual task a human can.

AI has been integrated into many fields, including healthcare, finance, transportation, and entertainment. AI is used for disease diagnosis, personalized medicine, and drug development in healthcare. In finance, AI is used for fraud detection, risk assessment, and investment management. In transportation, AI is used for self-driving cars, traffic management, and logistics optimization. In entertainment, AI is used for personalized content recommendations, chatbots, and virtual assistants.

There are many reasons why people are investing in AI. One of the most significant is the potential for AI to transform industries and create new markets. AI can reduce costs and increase productivity by automating tasks and improving efficiency. In addition, AI has the potential to improve decision-making by analyzing vast amounts of data and providing insights that would be difficult or impossible for humans to identify.

Another factor driving investment in AI is the promise of improved quality of life. AI has the potential to revolutionize healthcare by enabling more accurate diagnoses and personalized treatments. It can also improve education by providing personalized learning experiences for students.

AI has come a long way since its inception, and its integration into different fields has significantly impacted our lives. While concerns about the future of AI are valid, it is important to acknowledge that AI is still limited by its programming and training. Inevitably, AI will become the next technological step, and as it does, it will continue to revolutionize how we live, work, and interact with technology.

CHAPTER 1:
YOUR LAW FIRM AND AI

Artificial Intelligence (AI) has been a buzzword in various industries, and the legal sector is no exception. The increasing use of AI in law firms has transformed how legal services are delivered. People have started saying that AI will replace professionals like lawyers. However, I hope to convince you that AI will replace lawyers who won't use artificial intelligence.

The Role of AI in Law Firms

AI has played a significant role in the legal industry by automating repetitive and time-consuming tasks, enabling lawyers to focus more on complex and strategic legal work. Some of the areas where AI has been applied in law firms include:

Legal Research and Analysis

Legal research is an essential part of legal work and is time-consuming. AI-powered tools have made legal research faster and more efficient. AI-powered tools can analyze vast amounts of legal data in seconds and provide insights that would have taken lawyers hours or days to discover.

Using AI will enable attorneys to complete a majority of discovery in litigation cases. Identifying similar injuries, injury histories, sample cases, and evaluating future loss of income and disabilities caused by simple accident or work-related injuries.

Emotional stress is caused by the work environment, psychoanalysis of events, future mental disorders, and the effect of such events on future life and work environments.

These are only some samples of AI's impact on research and analysis.

Contract Review and Analysis

AI-powered contract review tools can analyze and identify risks in legal contracts, enabling lawyers to focus on critical areas that require their attention. These tools can also extract essential information from contracts and organize it in a structured way, making it easier for lawyers to analyze and make decisions.

AI is most effective in identifying all risk factors with each contract by having access to millions of samples, analyzing each term in the contract, and examining all possible scenarios for the bridge of the contract. Simultaneously, it would identify all the risk factors and create a term that can minimize the ability of other parties to break the contract or challenge the terms. This function is currently impossible to complete with human resources. All these functions described above can be done in minutes and not months.

You can submit a written contract to an AI engine and ask to be examined for all possible false and challenges. Then you can ask you to rewrite the contract to minimize the risk in each contract term. Recommending protection in contracts and write-ups.

Predictive Analytics

AI-powered predictive analytics tools can help lawyers to predict the outcome of legal cases by analyzing vast amounts of data from previous cases. Predictive analytics can help lawyers to make informed decisions and advise clients accordingly.

Predictive analysis done by AI system could include:

- Future Injuries
- Future Disabilities

- The estimated cost of litigation
- Percentage of success based on the merit of the case.
- The estimated settlement value is based on historical data, Case, Jury, Judge, and all other factors.

E-Discovery

AI-powered e-discovery tools can analyze large volumes of data and identify relevant information for legal cases. E-discovery tools can also help lawyers to reduce the time and cost of conducting discoveries.

What is discovery?

Collecting data from various sources, serving requests and subpoenas, receiving and analyzing data, and creating a summary for attorneys. Well, this is a core value of an AI system. Access all types of information worldwide, identify the relevant data, compare data collected, and create the best summary report that any attorney can wish for. It will access the available data, generate the request for information letters, create and submit subpoenas, and do all the follow-ups. All in a matter of hours, not months.

These will include medical records, employment records, financial information, previous judgments, credit reports, and many other categories of data with no time or capacity limitations.

AI tools in law firms

Artificial intelligence (AI) is transforming the legal industry in ways that were once unimaginable. From contract analysis to legal research, AI-powered tools are helping lawyers improve their daily routines. These tools save them time and resources while increasing accuracy and efficiency.

Legal Research

Legal research is critical to a lawyer's daily routine, requiring them to build a strong case for their clients. This can be done by reviewing various case laws, statutes, and legal precedents. AI-powered tools can assist lawyers by performing the initial research and sorting relevant cases according to specific criteria, saving lawyers valuable time and effort.

One such AI-powered tool is ROSS Intelligence, which uses natural language processing (NLP) algorithms to understand legal documents and provide relevant case laws to lawyers. The tool can also track case updates and notify lawyers of any new developments that may impact their cases.

Another tool is LexisNexis, which uses machine learning algorithms to search vast legal information databases and provide relevant results to lawyers. The tool can also predict potential outcomes and help lawyers build stronger cases.

Finally, you have Westlaw Edge, which uses AI-powered algorithms to extract critical information from legal documents and provide insights to lawyers. The tool can also analyze briefs and identify potential risks and opportunities.

Contract Review

Contract review is another essential task that lawyers must undertake daily. Reviewing complex legal documents can be a time-consuming and tedious process. Still, AI-powered tools can help automate the process.

Contract review tools like Kira Systems use machine learning algorithms to extract critical information from contracts and identify potential risks and issues. This can save lawyers hours of manual review and reduce the likelihood of errors.

eBrevia is an AI tool that uses natural language processing (NLP) algorithms to extract essential information from contracts and identify potential risks and issues. The tool can also compare contracts to standard clauses and suggest changes.

Another contract review tool is Luminance, which uses machine learning algorithms to identify potential contract risks and opportunities. The tool can also provide insights into how contracts compare to industry standards and highlight potential issues.

Predictive Analytics

Predictive analytics can help lawyers gain insights into their clients' cases and make more informed decisions. AI-powered tools can analyze vast amounts of data and identify patterns and trends that may not be visible to the naked eye.

For example, tools like Lex Machina use machine learning algorithms to analyze millions of court documents to identify judges' behavior patterns and predict case outcomes. This can help lawyers prepare their cases accordingly and increase their chances of success.

Another tool is Premonition, which uses machine learning algorithms to analyze millions of court cases and identify patterns and trends. The tool can also predict potential outcomes and help lawyers build stronger cases.

Lastly, you have CaseText, which uses AI-powered algorithms to analyze case law and identify potential issues. The tool can also provide insights into how judges interpret cases and predict possible outcomes.

Document Management

Managing legal documents is another critical task that lawyers must perform daily. AI-powered tools can help automate this process, reducing the likelihood of errors and improving efficiency.

Document management tools like iManage use machine learning algorithms to classify and tag documents automatically. This makes it easier for lawyers to find the information they need quickly and efficiently.

Complex litigations like Mass Tort, Class Action consumer or employment, Copy Rights, and infringement involve massive document collection and management. Organizing such a document inventory that includes documents, pictures, Videos, Audio, and evidence is extremely time and resources intensive. The AI system is not limited; it can work 24/7 searching and collecting massive amounts of data, sorting, analyzing, identifying the level, or providing complete and accurate reports. Only firms with massive human and technology resources can try this. It would take an army and years to compile this level of information.

Virtual Assistants

AI-powered virtual assistants can help lawyers manage their daily schedules and tasks, allowing them to focus on more critical aspects of their work.

Virtual assistants like x.ai use NLP algorithms to schedule appointments and meetings automatically. This can save lawyers time and effort and reduce the likelihood of scheduling conflicts.

AI-powered tools are transforming the legal industry, allowing lawyers to perform their daily routines more efficiently and accurately. From legal research to contract review, predictive analytics to document management, AI is helping lawyers streamline their workflow, reduce the likelihood of errors, and improve efficiency. AI can enhance their daily routine, allowing them to provide better service to their clients.

AI-powered intake staff for any practice type. You are always worried about your intake staff being available, speaking multiple languages, asking the right questions, having all the right answers, and persuading the potential client to sign a retainer.

AI platform trained for each practice area has access to all possible questions asked by a potential client, has the most related and accurate answers, speaks all languages, can provide all possible scenarios for the client benefiting by retaining your firm, and much more.

Case Managers AI:

What do you expect your ideal Case Managers quality to be?

- ✓ Available always
- ✓ Speak multiple languages.
- ✓ Have a great understanding of the case.

- ✓ Know your client and make a connection.
- ✓ Collect all relevant documents and information about the case.
- ✓ Follow up with all events, calendaring, statutes, and appointments
- ✓ Know when to build the case and when to escalate the case.
- ✓ Organized
- ✓ Technology Savvy
- ✓ Great discipline to perform their tasks.
- ✓ Well, this is a very basic AI platform for Prelitigation.

Factors regarding integrating AI in your law firm

Some factors must be considered when using AI, so let's consider what you must take care of before implementing an AI tool.

Data Quality

Data quality is one of the most critical factors that must be considered when using AI. AI algorithms are only as good as the data they are trained on. The AI will produce inaccurate or biased results if the data is flawed or biased. Ensuring the data used to train AI algorithms is accurate, unbiased, and relevant is essential. It is also crucial to monitor and update the data as necessary.

Creating a data library (Domains, Libraries, Universities, Court documents) is critical to train your AI platform.

If you are utilizing pre-existing AI platform, test the documents and data created by the AI system. You may have to do additional data training for the AI engine for your type of practice area.

Understandability

Another chief factor that needs to be taken care of when using AI is understandability. AI algorithms can be complex and difficult to understand, making explaining how they arrived at their conclusions challenging. It is essential to ensure that AI algorithms are transparent and explainable so that lawyers and clients can understand how the AI arrived at its conclusions. This is particularly important in legal cases where the reasoning behind a decision is critical.

Ethics

Ethics is another critical factor that needs to be taken care of when using AI. AI algorithms can make decisions that have significant implications for individuals and society. It is essential to ensure that AI algorithms are designed and used ethically and do not discriminate against any particular group or individual.

Ethics requirements are different from state to state and practice by practice. You must ensure that AI platforms are trained in your state requirements and that ethical decisions or recommendations align with actual requirements.

You can always ask the AI system the question, but at the beginning of this phase, you have to verify the answer and give the AI a chance to correct itself and adjust to relevant conditions.

Security

Security is another crucial factor that demands attention when using AI. AI algorithms are only as secure as the systems they are running on. AI algorithms may be compromised if these systems are vulnerable to cyber-attacks. It is essential to ensure that AI algorithms are run on secure systems and that the data is protected from unauthorized access. It is also crucial to ensure that AI algorithms do not introduce new vulnerabilities into existing systems.

Human Oversight

Finally, human oversight is an essential factor to consider when using AI. While AI algorithms can be highly accurate and efficient, they can never entirely replace human judgment and expertise. Ensuring that human lawyers are involved in the decision-making process and have the final say in legal cases is essential. It is also crucial to ensure that lawyers are trained in using AI tools effectively and understand the limitations of these tools.

What's next for lawyers

The legal industry is ripe for revolution, and the next step in this transformation is the adoption of Artificial Intelligence (AI). AI has the potential to revolutionize the legal industry by providing lawyers and law firms with powerful tools to automate routine tasks, analyze vast amounts of data, and make more accurate and informed decisions. Let's explore the benefits of AI for lawyers and law firms and identify why adopting AI is the next evolutionary step for the legal industry.

Efficiency

One of the most significant benefits of AI for lawyers and law firms is increased efficiency. AI-based tools can automate many routine tasks, such as document review, legal research, and contract analysis. This automation can save lawyers and law firms significant time, allowing them to focus on more complex and strategic tasks. AI can also streamline workflow and collaboration, making it easier for lawyers to collaborate on cases and share information.

Accuracy

Another benefit of AI for lawyers and law firms is increased accuracy. AI-based tools can analyze vast amounts of data, including legal documents, case law, and contracts, and provide insights and recommendations that are more accurate than those provided by human lawyers alone. AI can also help to identify patterns and trends in legal data that human lawyers may miss, providing a more comprehensive and informed view of legal issues.

Cost Savings

AI can also provide significant cost savings for lawyers and law firms. By automating routine tasks, AI can reduce the need for human labor, which can be a significant expense for law firms. Additionally, AI-based tools can help lawyers and law firms identify cost-saving opportunities, such as identifying areas where legal processes can be streamlined or where legal risk can be reduced.

Enhanced Client Service

AI can also help lawyers and law firms provide better client service. Lawyers can offer their clients faster and more comprehensive service by automating routine tasks and providing more accurate and informed legal analysis. Additionally, AI can help lawyers identify legal risks and opportunities that may not have been apparent without AI-based tools, providing clients with a more comprehensive view of their legal situation.

Human resources are converting from the physical staff at the office to Virtual Staffing overseas and hybrid resources of Virtual Staffing with AI platform for the most efficient Law Organization.

I predict that most successful law organizations will be fully virtual with two types of AI platforms. Public AI platforms such as SaaS Systems and internally built and customized AI platforms provide the edge over the competition. The organizational chart will consist of humans and AI in one united organizational chart.

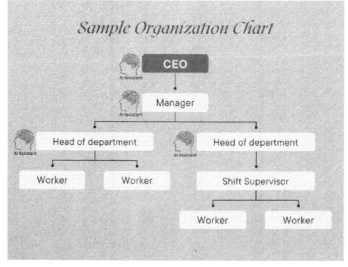

Competitive Advantage

Finally, adopting AI can provide law firms with a significant competitive advantage. Law firms that are early adopters of AI-based tools can differentiate themselves from competitors by delivering faster, more accurate, and more comprehensive legal services. Additionally, AI can help law firms identify and pursue new business opportunities, such as cross-selling services to existing clients or expanding into new legal practice areas.

Adopting AI is the next evolutionary step for lawyers and law firms. AI-based tools can increase efficiency, accuracy, and cost savings while enhancing client service and providing a competitive advantage. Law firms that are early adopters of AI-based tools can differentiate themselves from competitors and offer better client service. As the legal industry continues to evolve, the adoption of AI will be critical for law firms that want to stay ahead of the curve and provide the best possible service to their clients.

Let's prepare for the AI revolution!

Artificial intelligence (AI) has revolutionized various industries, including legal. Incorporating AI tools in your law practice can enhance efficiency, accuracy, and productivity.

However, careful planning is crucial to avoid legal, ethical, or practical issues.

To get started with AI implementation, begin by identifying your goals. Determine which areas of your practice could benefit from AI tools and prioritize your plans accordingly. Once you have a clear objective, research and evaluate AI tools that align with your goals, considering accuracy, efficiency, reliability, and cost factors.

Your team plays a critical role in effectively using AI tools; providing them with the necessary training is essential. Educate your team on how the AI tool works, how to interpret its output, and troubleshoot any issues. Additionally, ensure that they understand the limitations of the AI tool and how to complement it with human judgment.

AI tools have ethical and legal implications, and you must consider them before implementation. Ensure the AI tool aligns with your moral obligations, such as promoting fairness, impartiality, and non-discrimination. It should also comply with legal obligations like privacy and data protection laws.

Finally, monitor and evaluate the AI tool's performance regularly. Review the tool's output to ensure accuracy and reliability and evaluate its impact on your practice. Regularly monitoring and evaluating the AI tool will help you identify any issues early and make necessary adjustments.

Integrating AI into law practice is an exciting opportunity to enhance efficiency, accuracy, and productivity by planning carefully, training your team, considering ethical and legal implications, and monitoring the AI tool's performance. You can ensure it aligns with your objectives and ethical and legal obligations. Embrace the possibilities of AI to revolutionize your legal practice.

So, AI tools can enhance various aspects of your law practice, but you must plan for their implementation carefully. In the following chapters, you will learn how to integrate AI into different legal processes and hopefully convince you to start planning for AI integration.

AI Application for your law firm Online Presents:

- Client case anniversary outreach
- Monthly Newsletters
- SMS Marketing
- Review Collections
- Social Media Management
- Client referral Retention
- Website updates

- Creating well-edited videos
- Directory registrations
- Associations memberships
- Creating referral networks

AI resources for your law firm marketing:

- ✓ Identify the best target demographic.
- ✓ Best platforms to advertise with the best results.
- ✓ Cost of Client Acquisitions
- ✓ Ad contents (Text, Images, Massaging, Videos)
- ✓ Cost of lead generation
- ✓ Managing Conversion
- ✓ Calculating ROI
- ✓ Managing Budget and Seasonal targeting
- ✓ Competitive analysis with all online competitors

AI Application with Law Practice HR:

Recruiting based on all available online resources. Identify candidates, send questionnaires, evaluate candidates based on job requirements, score the candidate, set up interviews, and create offer letters.

- ✓ Track performance
- ✓ Evaluation criteria based on job descriptions.
- ✓ Evaluation based on market rates.
- ✓ Recommend career growth programs.

- ✓ Identify continuing education programs.
- ✓ Create evaluation criteria.
- ✓ Create an incentives program.
- ✓ Manage goals and quotas.
- ✓ Termination Notices
- ✓ Handbook development
- ✓ Corrective actions letters
- ✓ Separation Letters
- ✓ Release forms
- ✓ NDA's
- ✓ Independent contractors' agreements

AI Application in Law Firm Accounting:

Interface with a firm accounting system, bank statements, credit cards, Case Management Software, and all subscriptions. Provide the following services in real-time and accurately. Your accounting dream has come true.

- ✓ Track Case Cost
- ✓ Track Firm Budget vs. Actual
- ✓ Collection & Billing
- ✓ Payment reminders
- ✓ Cost Analysis per client/case
- ✓ Disbursement calculation
- ✓ Collection Letters

- ✓ Disbursement Letters
- ✓ Tax calculations
- ✓ Credit card expenses allocation and management

AI Application in Law Practice Technologies:

Analyze your technologies and compare them with published functions and features of technology providers to recommend the best customization and optimization for your practice. It is like having a team of technology experts at your service with no financial cost or incentives to recommend and help implement state-of-the-art solutions for your firm.

- ✓ Continuously search the web for new technologies targeted to improve and expand the functionality of the current system in use.
- ✓ Create competitive analysis for system upgrades and replacements.
- ✓ Create pros and cons for new solutions and optimizations.
- ✓ Identify the areas of practice that can utilize technology implementations.
- ✓ Create a roadmap for connectivity of all technology platforms.

AI Application in your practice area:

Personal Injury & Works Comp:

- ✓ Intake Process
- ✓ Case Management
- ✓ Document Collection
- ✓ Identify providers working on lien.
- ✓ Estimating case value
- ✓ Medical Bills Analysis
- ✓ Demand Writing
- ✓ Lien Reduction Analysis and recommendations
- ✓ Discovery Preparation and Analysis
- ✓ Trial Preparation (Deposition Summary)

Employment & Labor Law:

- ✓ Intake Process
- ✓ Case Management
- ✓ Document Collection
- ✓ Searching for all other possible plaintiffs
- ✓ Estimating case value
- ✓ Employment right violations based on each state
- ✓ Lost wages analysis
- ✓ Penalties calculations

- ✓ Earnings estimates are based on the market rate per location.
- ✓ Demand Writing
- ✓ Discovery Preparation and Analysis
- ✓ Trial Preparation (Deposition Summary)

Mass Tort & Class Action:

- ✓ Intake Process
- ✓ Plaintiffs targeting
- ✓ Case Management
- ✓ Document Collection
- ✓ Searching for all other possible plaintiffs
- ✓ Right violation based on each state
- ✓ Damages analysis
- ✓ Penalties calculations
- ✓ Identify all potential backfillings.
- ✓ Discovery Preparation and Analysis

Transactional Law:

Immigration, Bankruptcy, Family, Estate Planning, Real-Estate, Corporate formation, Contract Law, and many more;

This will be the most impacted type of practice with AI revolutions. Your firm collects client information to identify the best possible approaches (Type of Immigration forms,

Bankruptcy forms, Divorce Petitions, Contracts, Type of Estate Plans, and Type of corporations).

Based on your experience and client-provided information. Your firms identify the forms, complete the forms, review the client answers for the best results, and submit the applications with supported documents.

Then you do tracking for updates and provide the final results.

AI platforms can perform the same task at a fraction of the time and cost you can. It has access to all possible answers and the best results based on historical applications, loopholes, case studies, and success ratios based on filed applications. All necessary documents provide the best results based on each case. It is like taking college exams once you have all historical exams given by the same college professor with a prediction of all the new changes they would make. You will get an A+ in this class by using AI.

Only Litigate cases will require an experienced attorney, which is about 5% of cases filed.

Simply put, get with AI or change your career if your law firm is a Transaction Law Practice.

CHAPTER 2:
AI IN THE INTAKE PROCESS

The legal system is an essential aspect of society that helps maintain order and justice, and the initiation of any legal case starts with the intake process. The process of entering cases into the legal system is called the intake process. It is a crucial step in ensuring the proper functioning of the legal system.

The law intake process is the first step in initiating a case in the legal system. It involves submitting legal documents, such as a complaint or a petition, to the appropriate court or legal authority. The intake process requires the completion of specific forms and documentation that contain information about the parties involved, the nature of the case, and the legal claims.

The importance of the law intake process cannot be overstated. It is the gateway to the legal system, and any errors or omissions in the intake process can lead to delays, inefficiencies, and even the dismissal of a case. An accurate and efficient intake process ensures the prompt and fair handling of the cases, and that justice is served.

Efficiency is a critical aspect of the intake process. A well-designed and streamlined intake process can save time and resources, reduce costs, and improve the overall effectiveness of the legal system. In contrast, a poorly designed or inefficient intake process can result in backlogs, delays, and unnecessary expenses. For example, if the intake process is slow or convoluted, it can take longer for cases to be processed, thus resulting in delayed justice and increased costs.

Accuracy is equally essential in the intake process. Accurate information is critical in determining the appropriate legal course of action and ensuring parties receive a fair and just outcome. Inaccurate or incomplete information can result in incorrect judgments, legal decisions, and unfair outcomes. Therefore, ensuring that the intake process is accurate and complete is imperative.

A well-designed intake process is essential for a law firm to deliver quality legal services, but it is not possible without confronting challenges.

Challenge 1: Incomplete or Inaccurate Information

One of the primary challenges law firms face during the intake process is incomplete or inaccurate information. Incomplete information can result in delays, additional work, and increased costs. False information can lead to incorrect legal advice or even a lost case. To overcome this challenge, law firms must implement a process for verifying information and collecting missing details.

Challenge 2: Time Constraints

Time constraints are another significant challenge that law firms face during the intake process. The intake process is often time-sensitive, and law firms must act quickly to avoid missing deadlines. Law firms can overcome this challenge by implementing an automated intake system that streamlines the process and reduces the time required to complete it.

Challenge 3: Complexity

The intake process can be complex and confusing, especially for clients unfamiliar with the legal system. Law firms must ensure that the intake process is easy to understand and navigate for clients. To overcome this challenge, law firms should provide clear and concise instructions for completing the intake process and offer assistance and support to clients as needed.

Challenge 4: Technology Integration

The use of technology in the intake process can be a significant challenge for law firms, especially if the technology does not integrate with other systems used by the firm. Law firms must ensure that their intake process combines with their existing technology to avoid duplication of effort and reduce the risk of errors. To overcome this challenge, law firms should invest in technology solutions compatible with their current systems and offer robust integration capabilities.

Challenge 5: Staffing

Staffing is a significant challenge for law firms during the intake process. Law firms must ensure sufficient staff to handle the intake process efficiently. However, staffing can be costly, and law firms must balance their staffing needs with their budget. To overcome this ordeal, law firms can consider outsourcing some aspects of the intake process or implementing automation solutions that reduce the need for manual labor.

By implementing an AI system, you can have the AI solution powered by the human voice and video complete the entire Intake process by asking the right questions, answering the prospect questions accurately based on a vast knowledge base of data, predicting the follow-up questions, and retaining the client at the right time.

Benefits of AI in the law intake process

The intake process is a crucial step in the legal system, and it can be time-consuming, complex, and prone to errors. However, with the advancement of artificial intelligence (AI) technology, law firms can now automate many aspects of the intake process.

Increased Efficiency

One of the primary benefits of AI in the law intake process is increased efficiency. AI-powered intake systems can process large volumes of information quickly and accurately, reducing the time and effort required to complete the intake process. This increased efficiency allows law firms to handle more cases, reduce costs, and deliver faster and more efficient legal services to their clients.

Improved Accuracy

The intake process requires significant data collection and analysis, and errors or inaccuracies can lead to delays, additional work, and increased costs. AI-powered intake systems can analyze data quickly and accurately, reducing the risk of errors and ensuring that the information collected is complete and accurate. This improved accuracy allows law firms to provide more effective legal advice and ensure that their clients receive fair and just outcomes.

Streamlined Workflow

AI-powered intake systems can streamline the workflow by automating many of the manual processes involved in the intake process. This automation allows law firms to reduce the time and effort required to complete the intake process, freeing staff to focus on more complex legal tasks. This streamlined workflow can also help to reduce costs and increase overall efficiency.

Enhanced Client Experience

The intake process is often the first point of contact between a client and a law firm, and providing a positive experience for clients is essential. AI-powered intake systems can offer a more streamlined and efficient experience, reducing the time and effort required to complete the intake process. This enhanced experience can increase client satisfaction, referrals, and an improved reputation for the law firm.

Benefit 5: Data Analytics

AI-powered intake systems can also provide valuable data analytics to help law firms improve their intake process and legal services. These systems can analyze data from past cases, identify patterns and trends, and provide insights to help law firms improve their legal services, streamline their workflow, and increase efficiency.

Examples and functions of AI tools in the intake process

As technology advances, more law firms turn to artificial intelligence (AI) tools and software to streamline their intake process. These tools and software can automate many aspects of the intake process, increasing efficiency, improving accuracy, and enhancing the overall client experience. AI-powered programs can now ask the right questions and provide correct answers, improving the accuracy and efficiency of legal services. Let's explore some examples of AI tools and software for the law intake process.

Legal Research Tools

Legal research is a critical component of the legal process and can be time-consuming and tedious. AI-powered legal research tools can save time and improve accuracy by automatically analyzing case law, statutes, and other legal documents. These tools can also provide insights into legal trends and patterns, helping lawyers make more informed decisions.

Chatbots

Chatbots are AI-powered programs that can interact with clients and answer their questions. Chatbots can be integrated into a law firm's website or social media platforms, allowing clients to ask questions and receive answers quickly and efficiently. Chatbots can also be programmed to collect basic client information and schedule consultations, reducing the need for manual data entry.

Document Automation

Document automation software can help law firms create and manage legal documents quickly and efficiently. These tools can automatically generate standard legal documents based on client information, such as contracts and agreements. This automation can save time and reduce the risk of errors in the document creation process.

Natural Language Processing (NLP)

Natural language processing (NLP) is an AI technology that analyzes and understands human language. NLP tools can automatically extract key information from legal documents, such as contracts and agreements, and input it into a law firm's intake system. This automation can save time and reduce the risk of errors in data entry.

Predictive Analytics

Predictive analytics software can analyze past cases and predict the outcome of current cases. This technology can help law firms make more informed decisions about which cases to take on, how to structure their fees, and how to allocate resources. Predictive analytics can also help law firms identify trends and patterns in their cases. It allows them to provide more effective legal advice to their clients.

Virtual Assistants

Virtual assistants are AI-powered programs that can perform various tasks, such as scheduling appointments, setting reminders, and managing emails. Law firms can use virtual assistants to automate many of the administrative tasks involved in the intake process, freeing staff to focus on more complex legal tasks.

Contract Review Software

Contracts are an essential part of the legal process and reviewing them can be time-consuming and prone to errors. AI-powered contract review software can automate much of the contract review process, including analyzing contract language, identifying key provisions, and highlighting potential issues. This automation can save time and improve accuracy, ensuring a thorough and effective review of contracts.

AI tools and software offer law firms a wide range of benefits, including increased efficiency, improved accuracy, enhanced client experience, and valuable data analytics. Chatbots, document automation software, natural language processing, predictive analytics, and virtual assistants are examples of the many AI tools and software available to law firms. By leveraging these technologies, law firms can streamline their intake process, reduce costs, and deliver quality legal services to their clients. However, there are several things that you need to keep in mind.

Ethical and legal issues related to AI in law intake

The use of AI in law intake also raises ethical and legal issues that must be addressed. Let's explore some ethical and legal issues related to AI in law intake.

Bias

AI systems are only as unbiased as the data they are trained on. If the data used to train an AI system is biased, the system will be biased. This can result in unfair treatment of clients based on race, gender, or other factors. Law firms must ensure that their AI systems are trained on unbiased data and regularly audited for bias.

Privacy

AI systems can process large amounts of personal data, such as client names, addresses, and financial information. Law firms must ensure that this data is protected and that clients are informed about their data usage. Law firms must also ensure that their AI systems comply with data privacy regulations, such as the General Data Protection Regulation (GDPR) and the California Consumer Privacy Act (CCPA).

Accountability

AI systems can make decisions with significant legal consequences, such as predicting the outcome of a legal case or identifying potential clients. Law firms must ensure that their AI systems are transparent and accountable and that the decisions made by the system can be explained and challenged.

Professional Responsibility

Lawyers are responsible for providing competent and ethical representation to their clients. Using AI in law intake does not relieve lawyers of this responsibility. Law firms must ensure the ethical use of their AI systems and that lawyers have the training and knowledge to use them effectively.

Liability

AI systems can make mistakes, just like humans. Law firms must ensure they are not liable for any mistakes their AI systems make. Law firms must also ensure that clients are informed about the limitations of AI systems and that they understand that AI does not guarantee a particular outcome.

As the use of artificial intelligence (AI) in law intake continues to grow, it is essential to emphasize the importance of transparency and accountability. Transparency refers to the disclosure of how AI systems make decisions. In contrast, accountability refers to the ability to explain and justify these decisions. In addition, law firms must ensure compliance with data privacy laws to protect clients' personal information.

AI-powered intake systems offer significant benefits to law firms, including increased efficiency, improved accuracy, streamlined workflow, enhanced client experience, and valuable data analytics. By leveraging AI technology in the intake process, law firms can provide faster and more efficient legal services to their clients, reduce costs, and improve overall operations. As AI technology advances, AI's benefits in the law intake process will only increase, making it a crucial tool for law firms looking to remain competitive and deliver quality legal services.

CHAPTER 3:
AI IN OPERATION

A I has the potential to revolutionize the legal industry, making it more efficient, accurate, and accessible. If you don't keep up, you will be left behind. In the previous chapter, we discussed how AI tools can significantly reduce the time and effort required for legal research. They can analyze and summarize legal documents, identify relevant cases and statutes, and predict legal outcomes. Moreover, these tools can extract essential contract information, such as terms, obligations, and termination clauses, and flag potential risks or inconsistencies.

AI tools are also essential for maintaining due diligence in many legal operations. They can assist with due diligence by analyzing large volumes of data and identifying potential risks or compliance issues. Another important legal operation aspect is E-discovery.

E-discovery involves identifying, preserving, and collecting electronically stored information (ESI) for legal proceedings. AI tools can assist with e-discovery by analyzing and categorizing large volumes of ESI and identifying potentially relevant information.

AI is transforming the legal industry by making it more efficient, accurate, and accessible. AI is used in different law operations, from legal research and contract analysis to predictive analytics and virtual assistants. As AI technology continues to advance, it is essential for law firms to embrace these tools to remain competitive and provide the best possible service to their clients.

Data Analysis and Collection

Data analysis and collection are crucial aspects of the legal industry, and AI can significantly improve these processes. By analyzing vast amounts of data, AI can identify potential risks and predict the likelihood of success or failure in legal cases. AI can help law firms make informed decisions.

AI is revolutionizing law firms' operations, from predictive analytics and e-discovery to legal research and contract analysis. As AI technology continues to advance, it is essential for law firms to embrace these tools to remain competitive and provide the best possible service to their clients.

AI platforms can instantly search all available data sources, creating relevancy between the data sources, identifying the uniqueness of data to your case, and drawing summary recommendations instantly. Law practices with unlimited human resources cannot achieve this.

Walking to any trial with AI outcomes and recommendations will give you an amazing edge.

Data Analysis with any demand writing project would also justify higher demand values based on analysis of the short-term and long-term impact of injuries based on historical data on similar injuries and outcomes.

Identifying Demographics and Targeted Clients

Identifying demographics and targeted clients is essential to any successful business, including law firms. AI can help law firms identify their target clients and demographics more accurately and efficiently in today's digital age. Data collected from past clients, leads, online data, and data warehouses worldwide can assist your demographic targeting to a very exact target. No more guessing what demographic to target in what geographic area. You will have the most efficient demographic, expected conversions, and the value of each case retained.

Social Media Analytics

Since AI can analyze social media data to identify patterns and trends in user behavior, law firms can identify potential clients by analyzing this data based on user demographics, interests, and behavior, along with the platforms and the types of content they consume.

What AI can do for your firm social media:

- Identify trending topics in your practice area
- Identify your competition post and outcomes
- Create the most engaging social media content based on your demographics, state, practice, and target audience
- Can track all follower reactions to your post and optimize your future post for the best results
- Can create a series of posts to keep the follower engage
- Track your social media boost and recommend additional boosts for your post
- Automatically engage with your audience
- Guide your followers to further engagement
- Provide a comprehensive social media report

The Cost of Client Acquisitions

Let's examine the costs and returns of investing in AI tools and AI-based leads. Client acquisition is an essential part of any law firm. However, it can be costly and time-consuming, requiring significant investments in marketing and intake efforts. With the advancement of AI, law firms can now use AI-based leads to streamline client acquisition, reduce costs, and improve the return on investment (ROI).

Client Acquisitions with AI platform includes the following:

- Identify the lead sources
- Track lead cost
- Lead demographic
- Lead conversion
- Cost of client acquisitions
- Feed the results to the lead source to optimize the campaign
- Find other campaigns with similar results
- Calculate ROI by matching cases to CRM data and settlements

The ROI of Using AI-based Leads

AI-based leads can help law firms streamline the client acquisition process, reduce costs, and improve ROI. By using AI to identify potential clients and their characteristics, law firms can target their marketing efforts more effectively. It can result in higher conversion rates and a lower cost per lead. AI can also help law firms automate the lead nurturing process, allowing them to focus on high-value activities such as meeting with potential clients and providing legal services. AI-based leads can also help law firms improve the quality of their leads, resulting in higher conversion rates and ROI.

The cost of client acquisitions can be a significant challenge for law firms, requiring significant investments in marketing and intake efforts. However, AI-based leads can help law firms streamline client acquisition, reduce costs, and improve ROI. By using AI to identify potential clients and their characteristics, law firms can target their marketing efforts more effectively, resulting in higher conversion rates and a lower cost per lead. As AI technology continues to advance, it is essential for law firms to embrace these tools to remain competitive and provide the best possible service to their clients.

AI solutions can calculate your entire cost of operations, client acquisition cost, and division of cost per client and determine the following data:

- ROI on each type of case
- Average settlement cost
- Average time spent on clients/cases
- Hourly earnings per function and cases

AI and the Pre-Litigation Process

AI can be particularly beneficial in pre-litigation processes, such as evaluating completion dates and points. Pre-litigation processes involve all the steps a legal team takes before a case goes to court. These processes include gathering evidence, analyzing facts, and negotiating with opposing parties. Pre-litigation processes are time-consuming and require significant resources to be completed effectively.

AI can assist legal teams in streamlining pre-litigation processes by automating time-consuming tasks, such as data collection and analysis. AI can quickly analyze large volumes of data and provide valuable insights, which can help legal teams make informed decisions. For example, AI can analyze a client's contract history to determine which types of contracts have resulted in litigation. This information can be used to identify potential risks and help the legal team to mitigate them.

AI ability to provide the following automated task for your Pre-Litigation process:

- Identify Providers (Lien and Others)
- Set up appointments
- Confirm Appointments
- Collect Medical Records
- Store collected information into case management SW
- Analyze and summarize collected data
- Create summary recommendation
- Produce the case demand
- Create a chart of recommended lien reduction
- Create a disbursement table

Evaluating Completion Dates and Points

Completion dates and points are essential in pre-litigation processes, as they help legal teams determine a case's next steps. For example, completion dates ensure that all necessary evidence is collected before the deadline. Evaluation of completion dates and points can be challenging and time-consuming, particularly in complex cases.

AI can assist legal teams in evaluating completion dates and points by analyzing data and predicting outcomes. AI can analyze past cases and identify patterns to predict the likelihood of a case settling or going to trial. This information can help legal teams determine a case's next steps and allocate resources effectively.

AI can revolutionize the legal industry by automating time-consuming tasks and increasing efficiency. In pre-litigation processes, AI can help legal teams streamline tasks, such as data collection and analysis, and accurately evaluate completion dates and points. By leveraging AI technology, legal teams can improve their decision-making processes and provide better outcomes for their clients. As AI technology advances, legal teams must embrace these tools to remain competitive and provide the best possible service to their clients.

AI and injury cases

Medical records and bills are critical in personal injury cases, as they provide evidence of the injuries sustained and the costs incurred. However, collecting and analyzing this information can be time-consuming and complex, particularly when multiple medical providers and treatments are involved. This is where AI can be valuable, as it can assist in collecting and analyzing medical records and bills and anticipating future injuries and costs. We will examine how AI can be used in law operations to collect medical records and bills and anticipate future injuries and costs.

Collecting Medical Records and Bills

AI can assist legal teams in collecting medical records and bills by automating the process of requesting and organizing this information. For example, AI can generate a list of medical providers and contact information, request the necessary records and bills, and organize them into a centralized database for easy access by the legal team.

Analysing Medical Records and Bills

Once medical records and bills are collected, AI can analyze them to identify patterns and trends, which can help the legal team to build a stronger case. For example, AI can analyze the types of treatments received and the associated costs to anticipate future expenses and build a compensation case.

Anticipating Future Injuries and Costs

AI can also assist in anticipating future injuries and costs by analyzing data and predicting outcomes. For example, AI can analyze past cases with similar injuries and treatments to predict the likelihood of future complications or medical expenses. This information can be used to negotiate a settlement or build a compensation case.

AI can be valuable in law operations by collecting and analyzing medical records and bills and anticipating future injuries and costs. By leveraging AI technology, legal teams can streamline collecting and analyzing medical information and build more substantial client cases. As AI technology advances, legal teams must embrace these tools to remain competitive and provide the best possible service to their clients.

AI and Managing HR

In recent years, AI has become an increasingly popular tool for managing various human resources (HR) aspects. From employee training and development to cost analysis and benefits management, AI has the potential to revolutionize the way HR processes are managed.

Managing HR with AI

One of the primary benefits of AI in HR management is its ability to automate routine tasks, such as employee data entry and management. By using AI to manage HR processes, organizations can streamline their HR operations, reduce administrative costs, and improve the accuracy of their HR data. AI can also help to identify potential HR issues before they become major problems, allowing organizations to take proactive measures to address them.

Managing Benefits with AI

AI can also manage employee benefits, including health insurance, retirement schemes, and other programs. Organizations may identify the benefits employees value the most, are the most affordable, and are most likely to draw in and keep top talent by utilizing AI to evaluate employee data. With this information, businesses can create better benefits plans that cater to their workforce's requirements and save money.

Managing Employee Training and Development with AI

AI can also be used to manage employee training and development programs. By analyzing employee data, AI can identify skill gaps and training needs within the organization, allowing organizations to design more effective training programs. AI can also help track employee progress in training programs, identify areas where additional training is needed, and provide personalized learning experiences tailored to each employee's needs.

Cost Analysis with AI

Finally, AI can analyze the costs associated with HR processes and identify areas where costs can be reduced. By analyzing employee salaries, benefits, and other HR-related expenses, organizations can identify areas where they can save money without sacrificing the quality of their HR programs. AI can also forecast future HR-related costs, allowing organizations to better plan and budget for these expenses.

AI can potentially revolutionize how HR processes are managed within organizations. Automating routine tasks, improving data accuracy, and providing valuable insights into employee behavior and performance. AI can help organizations to design better HR programs that meet the needs of their employees and are more cost-effective for the organization. As AI technology evolves, it will likely become an essential tool for HR professionals in managing HR, benefits, employee training and development, and cost analysis.

CHAPTER 4:
AI IN MARKETING

In today's fiercely competitive business world, marketing has become essential for law firms to stay ahead of the competition. However, many law firms still believe that traditional reputation-building methods and acquiring clients are enough. The legal sector has been slower to embrace marketing compared to other industries. This is partly due to the nature of the profession, which is rooted in tradition and ethics. However, marketing has become increasingly important for law firms to remain relevant and competitive.

Why is marketing needed?

Legal sector marketing refers to promoting legal services to potential clients, building brand awareness, and establishing a positive reputation. This can include various activities such as advertising, networking, public relations, content marketing, and social media.

One of the primary benefits of marketing in the legal sector is that it helps law firms to differentiate themselves from their competitors. With so many law firms offering similar services, it's essential to have a unique value proposition that sets your firm apart. Effective marketing helps to establish your brand identity, highlighting your unique strengths and values and communicating them to potential clients.

Marketing also helps law firms to build trust and credibility with their clients. By showcasing your expertise, experience, and success stories, you can position your firm as a trusted authority in your practice area. This can be especially important for small law firms or solo practitioners who may not have the same level of name recognition as larger firms.

Another key benefit of marketing in the legal sector is that it can help to generate leads and acquire new clients. In today's digital age, potential clients increasingly turn to online search engines and social media platforms to find legal services. Law firms can increase their visibility and attract new clients by investing in digital marketing strategies such as search engine optimization (SEO), pay-per-click (PPC) advertising, and social media marketing.

In addition to attracting new clients, marketing can help retain existing ones. Law firms can establish a stronger connection with their clients and encourage repeat business by providing relevant and engaging content through newsletters, blogs, and social media.

Finally, marketing in the legal sector can help law firms to adapt to changing market conditions and stay ahead of the competition. By regularly monitoring market trends and adjusting your marketing strategy accordingly, you can ensure that your firm remains relevant and competitive.

Marketing with AI

Marketing, including the legal sector, has become essential to the business world. For law firms to remain competitive, they must invest in marketing strategies to differentiate themselves from their competitors, attract new clients, and retain existing ones. However, with the advancements in artificial intelligence (AI), law firms can now leverage technology to uphold their name in the public's eye.

Marketing requires a specialized team with years of experience in the field. For instance, developing effective marketing strategies requires market research, brand positioning, messaging, and communication expertise. This expertise is often beyond the scope of legal professionals who deliver legal services to their clients. Consequently, law firms must invest in a marketing team, which can be costly and time-consuming.

However, with the advent of AI, law firms can now leverage technology to enhance their marketing efforts. AI refers to the simulation of human intelligence processes by computer systems. AI can process and analyze vast amounts of data, identify patterns and trends, and make predictions based on the data. This makes it a valuable tool for law firms to improve their marketing strategies.

AI can help law firms with their marketing efforts by analyzing client data. Law firms can collect client preferences, behavior, and demographics data. AI can analyze this data to identify patterns and trends, providing insights into what clients want and how to target them effectively. This information can be used to develop personalized marketing campaigns that resonate with the client's interests and preferences.

AI can also help law firms to optimize their digital marketing efforts. AI can analyze website traffic data to identify the pages and content that generate the most engagement. This information can be used to develop content that is more likely to attract and retain visitors, improving the firm's search engine optimization (SEO) and online visibility.

AI can also be used to improve the efficiency and effectiveness of social media marketing. AI can analyze social media data to identify trending topics and keywords, which can be used to develop content that resonates with the audience.

AI can also automate social media posts, reducing the time and effort required to manage social media accounts.

AI can lead the marketing campaign

Artificial intelligence (AI) has transformed businesses' operations and revolutionized the marketing industry. AI has proven particularly useful in managing social media posts, website content, blogs, e-newsletters, client reviews, and other updates.

Social Media Management

Social media is an integral part of any business's marketing strategy. However, managing social media accounts can be a time-consuming and labor-intensive task. AI can help businesses streamline the process by automating social media posts, analyzing engagement, and providing insights on the most effective social media strategies.

With AI, businesses can automate creating and posting of social media content. AI-powered tools can generate social media posts based on the business's branding, tone of voice, and target audience. This can save businesses a significant amount of time and effort.

AI can also analyze engagement metrics such as likes, comments, and shares to identify the content that resonates best with the audience. This information can be used to adjust social media strategies and create more compelling content in the future.

Website Content Management

A company's website is the first point of contact for potential customers. It's imperative to keep the website updated with fresh and relevant content.

AI-powered tools can generate website content based on the business's branding, tone of voice, and target audience. This content can be optimized for search engines, making it easier for potential customers to find business online. AI can also analyze website traffic data to identify the pages and content that generate the most engagement. This information can be used to develop content that is more likely to attract and retain visitors.

Blog Management

Blogs are a valuable marketing tool for businesses to establish their expertise, connect with their audience, and drive traffic to their website. However, creating and managing a blog can be time-consuming and requires significant effort. AI can help businesses streamline the process by automating, creating, and optimizing blog content.

AI-powered tools can generate blog content based on the business's branding, tone of voice, and target audience.

This content can be optimized for search engines, making it easier for potential customers to find the blog online. AI can also analyze engagement metrics such as likes, comments, and shares to identify the content that resonates best with the audience. This information can be used to develop content that is more likely to attract and retain readers.

E-Newsletter Management

E-newsletters are an effective way for businesses to communicate with their audience and provide updates on their products and services. However, managing an e-newsletter can be challenging, especially if the company has an extensive subscriber list. AI can help businesses automate the process of creating and sending e-newsletters.

AI-powered tools can generate e-newsletter content based on the business's branding, tone of voice, and target audience. This content can be customized to the subscriber's preferences and interests, making it more engaging and relevant. AI can also analyze engagement metrics such as open and click-through rates to identify the most effective e-newsletter strategies.

Client Reviews Management

Client reviews are an essential part of a business's reputation. However, managing client reviews can be challenging, especially if the business has a large client base. AI can help businesses automate collecting, analyzing, and responding to client reviews.

AI-powered tools can collect and analyze client reviews from various platforms to identify common themes and sentiments. This information can be used to improve the business's products and services and respond to client feedback effectively. AI can also automate responding to client reviews, saving businesses time and effort.

Tweaking your official website

AI can help businesses analyze site visitors and trace customers' journeys to tweak their website and improve their online presence.

Understanding Site Visitors

Analyzing site visitors is crucial for businesses that want to improve their website's performance. AI can help enterprises to understand their site visitors by providing valuable insights into their behavior and preferences. This information can be used to improve the user experience and drive engagement.

With AI, businesses can analyze page views, bounce rates, time on site, and click-through rates. This data can be used to identify patterns and trends in visitor behavior, such as which pages are most popular, how long visitors stay on a page, and what actions they take before leaving the site.

By understanding their site visitors' behavior, businesses can optimize their websites to meet their needs better. For example, suppose visitors tend to leave the site after visiting a particular page. In that case, businesses can analyze that page and make changes to improve the user experience.

Tracing Customer Journeys

Tracing customer journeys is another crucial aspect of website analysis. AI can help businesses trace customers' journeys by providing insights into their behavior and preferences across multiple channels and touchpoints.

With AI, businesses can track customer interactions across various channels, such as social media, email, and chatbots. This data can be used to understand how customers engage with the business and what drives them to take specific actions.

Businesses can optimize their website by tracing customer journeys to meet their customers' needs at each journey stage. For example, suppose customers tend to drop off at the checkout page. In that case, businesses can analyze that page and make changes to improve the checkout process and reduce friction.

Tweaking the Website

By analyzing site visitors and tracing customer journeys, businesses can identify areas of their website that need improvement. AI can help businesses tweak their website by providing insights into which changes will likely significantly impact visitor behavior.

For example, suppose visitors tend to leave the site after a particular page. In that case, businesses can analyze that page and make changes to improve the user experience. This might include optimizing the page's layout, adding engaging content, or making the call-to-action more prominent.

Similarly, suppose customers tend to drop off at the checkout page. In that case, businesses can analyze that page and make changes to improve the checkout process and reduce friction. This might include simplifying the checkout process, offering alternative payment options, or providing more information about the product or service.

AI and reaching out to your customers

AI is transforming the way businesses operate and interact with their customers. By leveraging the power of AI, you can research your competitors and analyze customer profiles and other essential parameters. Let's look at how AI can help you gain a competitive edge.

Researching Your Competitors

One of the key advantages of AI is that it can help you research your competitors more effectively. AI algorithms can scan thousands of web pages, social media profiles, and other online sources to collect data on your competitors. This data can include information about their products, pricing strategies, marketing campaigns, and more.

Analyzing this data lets you gain insights into your competitors' strengths and weaknesses. You can use this information to develop more effective marketing strategies, identify new market opportunities, and create better products that meet your customers' needs.

Analysing Customer Profiles

Another area where AI can help is in analyzing customer profiles. By analyzing large amounts of customer data, AI algorithms can identify patterns and trends that might be difficult to detect using traditional research methods. For example, AI can analyze data from social media platforms, customer reviews, and other sources to identify what motivates customers to buy a particular product.

With this information, you can create more targeted marketing campaigns and develop products that meet the specific needs of your customers. By leveraging the power of

AI, you can gain a deeper understanding of your customer's inclinations and behaviors, which can help you stay ahead of the competition.

Other Essential Parameters

In addition to researching your competitors and analyzing customer profiles, AI can help you analyze other essential parameters. For example, AI can analyze your website traffic to identify where your customers are coming from, what pages they visit, and how long they stay on your site.

AI can also analyze your sales data to identify trends and patterns that can help you optimize your pricing strategies, improve customer retention, and increase sales. By using AI to analyze these essential parameters, you can better understand your business and make more informed decisions that can help you stay ahead of the competition.

Closing customers with AI

In today's digital age, having a strong online presence is vital to succeeding in the business world. One of the most effective ways to do this is using pay-per-click (PPC) and SMS marketing campaigns. However, creating effective campaigns requires the use of relevant and effective keywords. This is where artificial intelligence (AI) can be a game-changer.

Understand Your Audience

Before you can begin creating effective keywords, it's important to understand your target audience. AI can help you analyze customer data, including demographics, behavior patterns, and search queries. Using this information, you can identify the keywords and phrases your target audience will most likely use when searching for your products or services.

Use AI-Driven Keyword Research Tools

AI-driven keyword research tools can be powerful when creating effective PPC and SMS marketing campaigns. These tools use sophisticated algorithms to analyze data from various sources, including search engines, social media platforms, and industry-related websites, to identify relevant keywords to attract the right audience.

Some popular AI-driven keyword research tools include Google Keyword Planner, SEMrush, Ahrefs, and Moz Keyword Explorer. These tools can help you identify the search volume, competition, and relevance of specific keywords, allowing you to make informed decisions when creating your marketing campaigns.

Utilize Natural Language Processing (NLP)

Natural language processing (NLP) is a subfield of AI that deals with the interaction between human language and computers. It allows machines to understand, interpret, and generate human language, making it a valuable tool for keyword research.

NLP algorithms can analyze the meaning and context of search queries to identify relevant keywords and phrases. This can help you create more effective campaigns that target the intent of your customers rather than just their specific search terms.

Track and Optimize Your Campaigns

Finally, tracking and optimizing your PPC and SMS marketing campaigns is critical to ensure that they are generating the desired results. AI can help you analyze your campaign data in real time, including click-through rates, conversion rates, and other metrics.

Using AI-driven optimization tools, you can identify the most effective keywords and adjust your campaigns accordingly. This can help you achieve a higher return on investment (ROI) and maximize the impact of your marketing efforts.

In conclusion, AI can be a powerful tool for creating effective keywords for PPC and SMS marketing campaigns. Using AI-driven keyword research tools, natural language processing, and tracking and optimizing your campaigns, you can create campaigns that attract the right audience, generate leads, and drive conversions. As AI continues to evolve and improve, it will become an even more valuable asset for businesses looking to improve their online presence and drive sales.

CHAPTER 5:
AI IN CASE LITIGATION

L itigation refers to the process of resolving disputes or conflicts through legal action. It typically involves a plaintiff, who initiates the lawsuit, and a defendant, who is being sued. Litigation can take many forms, including civil, criminal, and administrative litigation. It is an essential aspect of the legal system used to protect individual rights, enforce laws, and maintain social order.

Litigation is a crucial aspect of the legal system to resolve disputes and protect individual rights. Using AI in the litigation process can help lawyers work more efficiently, reduce costs, and make more informed decisions. AI technology will likely become an increasingly important tool for lawyers and legal professionals.

Different Scenarios for Pursuing Litigation

Litigation can be pursued in many scenarios, including:

Contract disputes

When one party breaches a contract, the other party can seek damages.

Personal injury cases

When someone is injured due to the negligence of another party, litigation can be pursued to seek compensation.

Employment disputes

Litigation can be pursued in discrimination, wrongful termination, or wage disputes.

Intellectual property disputes

Litigation can be pursued to protect patents, trademarks, and copyrights.

How AI can Help in the Litigation Process:

The use of AI in the legal industry has grown significantly in recent years. AI can be used to assist lawyers in various aspects of the litigation process, including:

Case Analysis:

A crucial step in the legal process is case analysis. Lawyers must examine cases to create arguments and determine the appropriate legal methods. Lawyers can examine cases more effectively and precisely with AI-powered technologies. AI, for instance, may spot trends and connections across cases, which can aid attorneys in crafting powerful legal defences. AI can also evaluate legal papers and case law to find pertinent data and precedents.

Discovery Process:

Parties to a case exchange information and evidence throughout the discovery process. The process can be time-consuming and expensive, especially when dealing with big data. The discovery process can be sped up using AI-powered systems that automatically recognize and classify pertinent documents. AI, for instance, may recognize privileged papers, obfuscate sensitive data, and classify documents according to relevance.

Data Collection:

Data collection is a critical aspect of legal proceedings. Lawyers must collect and analyse data to build a case, identify patterns, and make informed decisions. AI can collect and analyse large volumes of data quickly and efficiently. For example, AI-powered tools can search social media platforms and online databases for relevant information. AI can also be used to analyse data from various sources, including financial records, medical records, and other documents.

Historical Precedents:

Historical precedents refer to past legal decisions that serve as a basis for future decisions. Lawyers must know historical precedents to make informed legal arguments and decisions. AI can be used to analyze large volumes of legal documents and case law to identify relevant historical precedents. For example, AI-powered tools can analyze court decisions and identify patterns and trends.

Document review

AI-powered tools can review large volumes of documents quickly and accurately. This can save lawyers significant time and money and reduce the risk of errors.

Predictive analytics

AI can be used to analyze case data and predict outcomes. This can help lawyers make more informed decisions and develop more effective litigation strategies.

E-discovery

AI can be used to search electronic documents for relevant information. This can be particularly useful in cases where there are large volumes of electronic data to review.

Legal research

AI-powered tools can be used to conduct legal research quickly and efficiently. This can help lawyers stay up to date on the latest legal developments and precedents.

Contract analysis

AI can be used to review and analyze contracts quickly and accurately. This can help lawyers identify potential risks and opportunities.

AI in different types of cases

Let's see how lawyers can use AI in different cases, such as injuries, medical treatment, loss of income, etc.

Injuries

AI can help attorneys in a variety of ways in personal injury cases. For instance, AI-powered technologies can examine medical reports and records to assist lawyers in finding pertinent data and crafting strong legal cases. To assist lawyers in determining the proper compensation, AI can also analyze data connected to the accident, such as the location and severity of the injury.

Medical Treatment

In cases where medical treatment is a factor, AI can analyze medical records and identify potential issues. For example, AI-powered tools can analyze medical records to identify potential malpractice cases. AI can also be used to analyze data related to medical treatment, such as the cost and effectiveness of various treatments, to help lawyers make informed decisions.

Loss of Income

AI is capable of analyzing financial data to calculate the right compensation in situations when there has been an income loss. AI-powered systems, for instance, can examine financial records to estimate the worth of lost wages or company revenues. AI may also evaluate economic data to assess how a loss of income will affect a person or firm.

Insurance Claims

AI is capable of analyzing insurance claims and spotting possible fraud or discrepancies. AI-powered technologies, for instance, can analyze insurance claims to find trends and similarities between claims. To assist lawyers in creating strong legal arguments, AI can also be used to evaluate data about insurance claims, such as the location and frequency of claims.

Legal Research

AI can be used to conduct legal research quickly and efficiently. For example, AI-powered tools can analyze case law and identify relevant legal precedents. AI can also analyze legal documents, such as contracts and agreements, to identify potential legal issues.

AI in different stages of litigation

Artificial intelligence (AI) is increasingly becoming valuable for lawyers in trial preparation, argument, and closing arguments. AI can help lawyers work more efficiently, reduce costs, and make more informed decisions.

Trial Preparation

AI can be used to assist lawyers in trial preparation in various ways. AI can also analyze legal documents, such as contracts and agreements, to identify potential legal issues. Additionally, AI can help lawyers organize and manage large volumes of data and documents, making it easier to find relevant information.

Argument

AI can be used to help lawyers create strong legal arguments. Artificial intelligence (AI)-enabled technologies can examine legal facts and forecast how a judge or jury could find in a certain case. This can aid attorneys in creating arguments that have a better chance of winning. AI can also help lawyers create counterarguments by spotting potential flaws in the other side's arguments.

Closing Arguments

AI can be used to assist lawyers in crafting persuasive closing arguments. AI-powered tools can analyze data related to the case, such as witness testimony and expert opinions, and identify key themes and arguments. AI can also analyze the judge or jury's responses to previous arguments to help lawyers refine their closing arguments.

Challenges and Considerations:

While AI can be useful for attorneys during trial preparation, presentation, and closing arguments, there are also difficulties and things to remember. Making sure that the use of AI in the legal system complies with ethical and legal requirements is one of the major problems. Ensuring AI is used ethically, responsibly, and without jeopardizing the judicial system's integrity is crucial.

The potential for AI to reinforce prejudices and inequality in the legal system is another factor to consider. Assume, for instance, that AI is trained on data that contains biases or inequalities. In that case, its analyses and projections might maintain those biases. It is crucial to guarantee that AI is trained on objective data and that its forecasts are understandable and transparent.

AI in predicting the outcome of cases

Predicting a case's outcome has always been difficult in the legal profession. To make wise conclusions, lawyers and other legal experts examine a wide range of material, including prior cases and judicial judgments. Yet, the development of artificial intelligence (AI) has made it easier than ever to predict the outcome of a case.

Lawyers and other legal professionals can utilize AI to examine data from previous cases and judicial opinions to better comprehend how judges have ruled in comparable instances. Predictive models can be developed using this technique to help attorneys evaluate the prospects for success for their clients.

Machine learning is one method by which AI can forecast a case's conclusion. Machine learning algorithms can analyze large volumes of data from prior cases and court decisions, which can be used to build prediction models. These models can forecast how new cases will turn out with the information. The immense amount of data that can be used to train machine learning algorithms allow them to discover patterns people might overlook.

Natural language processing is another way AI can aid with case direction prediction (NLP). The judges' main legal concepts, defences, and justifications can be found using NLP to examine the text of previous cases and judicial judgments. Based on the concepts and arguments raised in the case, this analysis can be used to develop models that forecast a judge's likely decision.

AI can also be used to examine public opinion and data from social media. Lawyers can use AI to examine social media data and determine how the public feels about a particular case. Using this information to forecast how the public will respond to the result may affect the case outcome.

By analyzing large amounts of data, creating predictive models, and analyzing social media data, AI can help lawyers and legal professionals make informed decisions. While AI cannot replace the human touch, it can help streamline the decision-making process and provide valuable insights into the direction of a case. With AI's continued development, its use in the legal industry will likely only increase in the coming years.

Using AI as a legal assistant

The legal system can be a complex and daunting world to navigate, with many variables that can influence the outcome of a case. However, with the emergence of Artificial Intelligence (AI) technology, it is now possible to analyze factors such as jury behavior, case costs, and deposition questions with greater precision and accuracy.

One of how AI can be used to analyze jury behavior is through sentiment analysis. Sentiment analysis involves using natural language processing (NLP) algorithms to analyze potential jurors' language in online forums or social media posts. This can provide valuable insights into the attitudes and biases of potential jurors and help lawyers and legal professionals identify those who may be unsuitable for a particular case.

AI can also be used to analyze case costs. By examining past cases and legal precedents, AI algorithms can create predictive models to help lawyers and legal professionals estimate a case's potential costs. This can be especially useful when dealing with complex cases that involve multiple parties and extensive discovery processes.

In addition, AI can be used to analyze deposition questions. Depositions are a key part of the legal process and can often be lengthy and complex. AI algorithms can analyze deposition questions and answers to identify key themes and patterns that can help lawyers and legal professionals to build a more compelling case.

One example of AI being used to analyze deposition questions is predictive coding. Predictive coding involves using machine learning algorithms to analyze large volumes of deposition data to identify key documents and information. This can help lawyers and legal professionals quickly identify relevant information and build a more persuasive case.

AI preparing your arguments and counterarguments

Lawyers and legal professionals spend countless hours analyzing past cases and legal precedents to identify the most effective arguments and anticipate potential counterarguments. However, with the emergence of Artificial Intelligence (AI) technology, it is now possible to prepare for arguments and counterarguments more efficiently and accurately than ever.

One way in which AI can help prepare for arguments and counterarguments is through predictive modeling. By analyzing large amounts of data from past cases and legal precedents, AI algorithms can identify patterns and predict the likelihood of success for different arguments. This can help lawyers and legal professionals to determine the most effective arguments to make in a given case and anticipate potential counterarguments.

AI can also be used to analyze the language used by opposing counsel in past cases. By analyzing the language used by opposing counsel in past cases, AI algorithms can identify the key arguments and counterarguments used by the opposition. This can help lawyers and legal professionals to prepare a more effective response to potential counterarguments and build a stronger case overall.

In addition, AI can be used to analyze the language used by judges in past cases. By analyzing the language used by judges in past cases, AI algorithms can identify the key factors that influenced their decisions. This can help lawyers and legal professionals to anticipate how judges are likely to rule in a given case and prepare more effective arguments accordingly.

AI and the litigation process in a nutshell

By facilitating different parts of legal proceedings, AI has the potential to revolutionize the legal sector. Lawyers can work more productively, spend less money, and make better choices using artificial intelligence (AI) in case analysis, the discovery process, data collection, and historical precedents. The importance of AI technology for lawyers and other legal professions is anticipated to increase as it develops.

AI has the potential to revolutionize the legal sector by supporting lawyers in a variety of tasks. Lawyers can operate more effectively, spend less money, and make better decisions by utilizing AI in various instances involving injuries, medical care, lost wages, and insurance claims. The importance of AI technology for lawyers and other legal professions is anticipated to increase as it develops.

CHAPTER 6:
AI IN LAW PRACTICE PROCESS AUTOMATION

AI is still in its infancy when it comes to the legal industry. However, law firms that integrate AI into their practices will have the edge over their competitors.

The legal industry is a dynamic and constantly evolving field dealing with various legal issues. The sector involves a lot of manual work, such as preparing legal documents, contracts, and agreements. The industry has witnessed a significant transformation in recent years with technological advancements. Automation has become a critical component of the legal sector, and its importance cannot be overemphasized.

Benefits of Automation

One of the primary benefits of automation in the legal industry is the ability to streamline repetitive tasks. By automating specific legal processes, lawyers and other legal professionals can save significant time and reduce the likelihood of errors. Automation can also improve accuracy, efficiency, and productivity. These are critical factors in the legal industry, where tight deadlines and mistakes can have severe consequences.

Another benefit of automation in the legal industry is cost savings. By automating specific tasks, law firms can reduce the need for manual labor, which can significantly lower operating costs. Automation can also help firms allocate better resources, leading to higher profitability.

Automation can also help the legal industry to improve access to justice. Legal services can be provided more efficiently and cost-effectively by automating certain legal processes. This can help to increase access to justice for low-income individuals and those who might not be able to afford legal representation.

Document management is one of the key areas where automation has been particularly beneficial in the legal industry. Document management is a critical function in the legal industry, and it involves handling and storing large volumes of legal documents. With automation, documents can be scanned, indexed, and stored electronically, making them easier to retrieve and manage. This can save significant time and reduce the risk of errors and loss of essential documents.

In addition to document management, automation has also been instrumental in contract management. Contract management involves creating, storing, and managing legal contracts. With automation, legal professionals can create templates for standard contracts customized for specific clients, reducing the risk of errors in the contract creation process.

AI and automation in the legal sector

In recent years, artificial intelligence (AI) and automation have profoundly impacted many industries, including the legal sector. From document review and contract analysis to legal research and case management, AI and automation have made many processes in the legal industry more convenient and efficient. Let's see some of the ways that AI and automation have transformed the legal industry.

Document Review and Analysis

One of the primary benefits of AI and automation in the legal industry is the ability to streamline and automate routine tasks. For example, document review is necessary for many legal matters, but it can be tedious and time-consuming for attorneys and paralegals.

However, AI automation can automate this work, allowing attorneys and legal professionals to focus on more complex tasks. AI-powered document review tools can analyze vast amounts of data quickly and accurately, flagging relevant information and reducing the time and effort required to review documents manually. This technology has been particularly helpful in litigation, where large volumes of documents are often involved, improving document review accuracy and consistency.

Due Diligence and Discovery

In addition to document review, AI and automation can also be used in due diligence and discovery. Due diligence is investigating a company or organization before a merger or acquisition. At the same time, discovery involves the collection and review of relevant documents in the course of a legal proceeding. Both processes can be time-consuming and costly, but AI and automation can help streamline these tasks by quickly and accurately identifying relevant documents and information.

Contract Review

Another area where AI and automation have significantly impacted is contract analysis. Contract review can be complex, and minor errors or oversights can have significant consequences. AI-powered contract analysis tools can help quickly identify potential contract issues, including missing clauses, discrepancies, and potential liabilities. These tools can also help automate contract drafting, making the process more efficient and accurate.

Legal Research

Legal research is another area where AI and automation can be beneficial. Researching case law and legal precedents can be daunting, requiring hours of reading and analysis. With vast amounts of legal data and information, AI and automation tools can quickly and efficiently search and analyze this data. This will allow attorneys to find relevant cases, statutes, and other legal materials more rapidly and efficiently, improving the accuracy and quality of legal research.

Case Management

AI and automation have also helped make case management more efficient in the legal industry. Software tools can track deadlines, manage case files, and automate many administrative tasks, allowing lawyers to focus on providing legal advice and advocacy. This technology can help law firms manage their workload more effectively and deliver better results to their clients.

Risk Assessment and Compliance

Finally, AI and automation can also be used in risk assessment and compliance. With the ever-increasing complexity of regulations and compliance requirements, it can be difficult for organizations to stay up-to-date and ensure compliance. AI and automation tools can help automate compliance tasks, such as monitoring potential regulatory violations, tracking regulation changes, and identifying potential risk areas. This can help organizations stay in compliance and avoid costly penalties and legal issues.

As technology continues to evolve, we will likely see even more innovative applications of AI and automation in the legal industry in the future.

AI and automating quality assurance

Artificial intelligence (AI) can potentially transform many aspects of a firm, including customer relationship management (CRM), communication automation, KPIs analysis, and lead management. By leveraging the power of AI, organizations can gain valuable insights, automate processes, and improve efficiency, ultimately driving better firm outcomes.

CRM

CRM is a critical aspect of any firm that wants to stay competitive and retain customers. AI can help firms set up and optimize their CRM systems by providing insights into customer behavior, preferences, and needs. AI tools can analyze customer data to identify patterns and trends, allowing firms to tailor their marketing and sales strategies to meet their customers' needs better. AI can also automate many aspects of CRM, such as lead scoring and prioritization, to help firms focus their efforts on the most promising prospects.

Communication Automation

Communication automation is another area where AI can be helpful. AI-powered chatbots can provide customers with personalized support and assistance 24/7, freeing human agents to focus on more complex tasks. Chatbots can also analyze customer inquiries and provide relevant information, such as product recommendations or troubleshooting tips, in real time. This improves the customer experience and helps firms save time and resources.

KPIs Analysis

Key performance indicators (KPIs) are critical metrics that firms use to measure their success and track progress toward their goals. However, analyzing KPIs can be a time-consuming and complex task. AI can automate KPIs analysis by gathering data from multiple sources, analyzing it, and presenting the results in an easily digestible format. This allows firms to identify areas of improvement and adjust their strategies accordingly quickly.

Lead Management

Lead management is tracking and managing leads throughout the sales funnel. AI can help automate many aspects of lead management, such as lead scoring, routing, and nurturing. AI-powered lead scoring algorithms can analyze customer data to determine which leads are most likely to convert, allowing firms to prioritize their efforts. AI-powered lead nurturing can also help firms stay in touch with leads and provide them with relevant information and offers to keep them engaged.

By leveraging AI tools and algorithms, firms can gain valuable insights, automate processes, and improve efficiency, ultimately driving better firm outcomes.

Selecting the best AI-based solution

As law firms embrace digital transformation, many are turning to automation and artificial intelligence (AI) solutions to improve efficiency, reduce costs, and gain a competitive edge. However, implementing automation and AI-based solutions requires careful planning and consideration.

Assessing Automation Needs

Before investing in any automation or AI-based solution, assessing your firm's specific needs and goals is essential. This involves identifying areas of your firm that most need automation, as well as determining which processes can be automated without negatively impacting the quality of your products or services. Some key questions to consider when assessing automation needs include:

- ✓ What are the biggest pain points in your firm processes?
- ✓ What tasks take up the most time and resources?
- ✓ Which processes can be automated without compromising quality?
- ✓ What are your firm goals, and how can automation help you achieve them?

By answering these questions, you can better understand your firm's automation needs and develop a plan for implementing automation solutions with the most significant impact.

Finding the Right Vendor or Software

Once you have identified your automation needs, it is time to find the right vendor or software to implement your AI-based solutions. Here are some key considerations to keep in mind when evaluating potential vendors or software:

1. **Experience:**

   Look for vendors or software with a track record of successfully implementing automation and AI-based solutions in your industry.

2. **Customization:**

   Your automation needs may be unique to your firm, so look for vendors or software that offer customizable solutions.

3. **Integration:**

   Ensure the vendor or software can integrate with your existing systems and workflows to avoid disruptions to your firm processes.

4. **Support:**

   Look for vendors or software that offer comprehensive support and training to ensure a smooth implementation process.

5. Cost:

Evaluate the total cost of ownership, including upfront costs and ongoing maintenance and support fees, to ensure that the solution fits your budget.

It is also essential to conduct thorough research and evaluate multiple vendors or software options to ensure you find the best fit for your firm's needs.

Implementing automation and AI-based solutions can bring significant benefits to your firm. Still, it is essential to carefully assess your automation needs and find the right vendor or software to implement your solutions. By taking a strategic approach to automation implementation and working with experienced vendors or software providers, you can achieve greater efficiency, cost savings, and firm success.

Automation has become an essential component of the legal industry, and its importance cannot be overemphasized. By automating specific legal processes, law firms can save time, reduce errors, lower operating costs, and improve access to justice. The legal industry will continue to evolve, and automation will undoubtedly play a critical role in its transformation.

CHAPTER 7:
AI IN FINANCE

AI is changing almost every industry, making them faster and more efficient. In the legal industry, AI's impact is limited to aiding lawyers, finance, and accounting.

The legal sector is a complex industry that requires a wide range of financial expertise to manage effectively. We will focus on other finances essential in the legal industry, including budgeting, billing, and tax accounting.

Budgeting

Budgeting is an essential financial practice in the legal sector. Law firms need to manage their finances carefully to ensure they can cover expenses and remain profitable. Effective budgeting requires thoroughly understanding the firm's income, fees, and financial goals. Law firms must plan and budget expenses such as rent, salaries, benefits, and supplies. Budgeting for unexpected expenses, such as legal disputes, equipment failure, or emergencies, is also essential. Budgeting can help law firms stay on track financially and make informed decisions about investments and growth opportunities.

Billing

Billing is another critical financial practice in the legal sector. Law firms must accurately track their time and expenses and bill clients for their services. Billing practices can vary depending on the firm's size, area, of course, and client base. Law firms may bill clients hourly, on a flat fee basis, or through alternative billing arrangements. Effective billing practices require transparency, accuracy, and communication between the firm and its clients. It is essential to establish clear billing policies and procedures and to provide clients with detailed invoices that explain the services provided and the associated costs

Cash flow management

Cash flow management is crucial in any business, and the legal sector is no exception. Law firms must manage their cash flow effectively to have enough cash to pay their bills, employees, and other expenses. In the legal sector, cash flow management is essential since law firms often work on a contingency fee basis, which means they don't get paid until the case is settled or won. This can create a lot of uncertainty, and law firms need a robust cash flow management system to deal with this uncertainty effectively.

Investment management:

Investment management is crucial for law firms that manage client funds, such as trusts or estates. Law firms must manage these funds carefully, ensuring they are invested wisely and according to the client's wishes. Failure to do so can result in legal consequences and loss of client trust. Law firms can manage their clients' funds with investment advisors or financial experts.

Tax planning

Tax planning is critical for any business, and the legal sector is no exception. Law firms must comply with all tax laws and regulations, including income tax, payroll tax, and sales tax. Law firms can work with tax professionals to ensure they meet all tax obligations and take advantage of tax breaks or incentives.

Effective cash flow management, billing and collections, budgeting and forecasting, investment management, and tax planning are all essential to the financial health of a law firm. Law firms can work with financial experts and implement financial software to help them manage their finances more effectively and efficiently.

AI and forecasting cost and revenue

Artificial intelligence (AI) has significant in automating case cost, case forecasting, and revenue forecasting. We will talk about how AI can help automate these processes and the benefits that this can bring to law firms and legal practitioners.

Case Cost Automation

Managing case costs is one of the legal sector's most time-consuming and complex tasks. Law firms need to track expenses associated with a case, including lawyer fees, court costs, and other expenses. They must also ensure they bill their clients accurately and promptly to avoid cash flow problems. With AI, law firms can automate this process, saving time and reducing the risk of errors. AI can analyze data from past cases to predict the costs associated with current circumstances and help law firms identify potential cost overruns before they occur. This can help law firms manage their finances more effectively and improve profitability.

Case Forecasting Automation

Case forecasting is an essential task for law firms. It involves predicting the outcome of a case and the associated costs. Accurate case forecasting helps law firms make informed decisions about whether to take on a case. With AI, law firms can automate this process and improve the accuracy of their predictions. AI can analyze data from past cases to identify patterns and trends that can help predict the outcome of current cases.

Revenue Forecasting Automation

Revenue forecasting is crucial for law firms to have enough cash flow to meet their expenses. AI can help law firms automate this process and improve the accuracy of their predictions. AI can analyze data from past cases and identify patterns and trends that can help predict future revenue. This data can help law firms make better financial decisions, plan for the future, and improve profitability.

Benefits of AI for Law Firms' finances

Automating case cost, case forecasting, and revenue forecasting can benefit law firms and legal practitioners. First, it can save time and reduce the risk of errors. Manual processes are time-consuming and prone to errors, leading to inaccurate predictions and financial problems. With AI, law firms can automate these processes and improve their accuracy, saving time and reducing the risk of errors.

Second, it can improve the accuracy of predictions. AI can analyze vast data and identify patterns and trends humans may miss. This can help law firms decide which cases to take and improve their success rate. It can also help law firms manage their finances more effectively and improve profitability.

Finally, AI can help law firms stay competitive. As AI becomes more prevalent in the legal sector, law firms that do not embrace this technology risk falling behind. Law firms can remain competitive and provide better client services by automating case costs, case forecasting, and revenue forecasting.

By embracing this technology, law firms can save time, improve accuracy, and stay competitive. As AI continues to evolve, we can expect to see more applications of this technology in the legal sector, bringing even more benefits to law firms and practitioners.

Identifying Profitable Cases

Identifying profitable cases is crucial for law firms to ensure they have enough cash flow to meet their expenses. With AI, law firms can analyze data from past issues and identify patterns and trends that can help predict the outcome of current cases. This can help law firms decide which cases to take on and which to avoid. AI can also analyze financial data to identify and prioritize the most profitable cases.

AI can help law firms identify profitable cases by analyzing data from various sources, including court records, financial records, and social media. They can analyze this data and provide insights into the most profitable cases, which can help law firms allocate resources more effectively and improve profitability.

Reduced Risk

Identifying the best profitable cases and the time required to conclude them is about profitability and reducing risk. Using AI algorithms, law firms can analyze data to identify potential risks and challenges associated with a particular case, helping them make more informed decisions about which cases to take and how to approach them. This can reduce the risk of taking on a case that may not be profitable or too challenging to win, thereby improving the firm's overall profitability.

Better Resource Allocation

Using AI to identify the best profitable cases and the time required to conclude them can help law firms allocate their resources more effectively. AI algorithms can help firms identify cases that require more resources and prioritize them accordingly. They can help law firms give their resources effectively and efficiently, improving profitability.

Improved Client Service

Using AI to identify the best profitable cases and the time required to conclude them can help law firms provide better client service. By quickly and accurately identifying the most profitable cases, law firms can focus on providing high-quality legal services to their clients, improving their satisfaction, and increasing their likelihood of referring other clients to the firm.

Using AI to cut expenses and increase efficiency

Efficiency is key in any business, and the legal industry is no exception. Law firms constantly seek ways to reduce costs and streamline their processes to provide better client service. One way to achieve this goal is to determine cost-saving practices and reduce the number of steps to conclude cases quicker.

Automate Routine Tasks

Automating routine tasks is one of the most effective ways to reduce costs and save time. Law firms can use software tools to automate document preparation, filing, and scheduling, among other tasks. By automating these tasks, law firms can reduce the time and resources required to complete them, allowing them to focus on more critical tasks such as case analysis and client communication.

Use Cloud-Based Services

Cloud-based services such as document management systems and case management software can help law firms save time and money. These services allow law firms to store and access case-related documents and information online, eliminating the need for physical storage space and reducing the risk of lost or damaged files. Additionally, cloud-based services can help law firms collaborate with clients and other stakeholders more quickly and efficiently.

Reduce the Number of Steps

Law firms can also save time and money by reducing the steps required to conclude cases. For example, law firms can simplify their intake process using online forms or questionnaires to collect client information. They can also streamline communication processes using email templates and pre-written responses to common client inquiries.

Use Data Analytics

Data analytics can help law firms identify cost-saving opportunities and improve their processes. By analyzing case outcomes, staffing levels, and other metrics, law firms can identify areas where they can reduce costs and improve efficiency. For example, data analytics can help law firms determine which cases are most profitable and which staffing levels are most effective.

Continuously Review and Improve Processes

Finally, law firms should continuously review and improve their processes to ensure they operate efficiently. Law firms should regularly evaluate their operations to identify bottlenecks and inefficiencies and implement strategies to address them. This can include training staff on new software tools, simplifying processes, or redesigning workflows.

Using AI to manage staff time spent on cases

The legal industry is known for its high-pressure environment, with attorneys and staff members working long hours to ensure that cases are handled effectively. However, managing staff time effectively can be challenging, especially when dealing with many cases simultaneously. Fortunately, advances in artificial intelligence (AI) have made it possible to streamline staff time management, increasing efficiency and productivity in the legal industry.

One of the most significant challenges facing law firms is managing staff time. Attorneys and support staff may be working on multiple cases simultaneously, each with its unique set of demands and deadlines. Keeping track of who is working on what, when tasks are due, and how much time is spent on each case can be overwhelming, especially for larger firms.

AI can help by automating many of these tasks. For example, AI-powered case management systems can automatically assign tasks to staff members based on their skills and availability, ensuring that work is distributed evenly and efficiently. These systems can also track the progress of each task, alerting staff members when a deadline is approaching, or a task has been completed.

Another way that AI can be used to manage staff time is by analyzing data to identify patterns and trends. For example, AI-powered time-tracking systems can analyze how much time is spent on each task and provide insights into how staff members can work more efficiently. This data can also identify which cases take up the most time and resources, allowing firms to allocate their resources more effectively.

AI can also automate many routine administrative tasks, such as scheduling meetings and sending reminders, freeing staff members to focus on more complex tasks, such as legal research and drafting documents. By automating these tasks, law firms can reduce the time staff members spend on administrative work, increasing productivity and efficiency.

In addition to these benefits, using AI to manage staff time can also help law firms to reduce costs. By automating routine tasks and identifying areas where staff members can work more efficiently, firms can reduce the time and resources required to complete each case. This, in turn, can lead to cost savings for both the firm and its clients.

Of course, there are also challenges associated with implementing AI in the legal industry. One of the biggest challenges is ensuring staff members are comfortable using these new technologies. To overcome this, law firms may need to provide training and support to help staff members get up to speed with the new systems.

Another challenge is ensuring that AI-powered systems are accurate and reliable, which requires robust testing and quality control processes to ensure the systems work as intended and provide accurate data.

Despite these challenges, the benefits of using AI to manage staff time in the legal industry are significant. By automating routine tasks, identifying areas where staff members can work more efficiently, and analyzing data to identify patterns and trends, law firms can increase productivity, reduce costs, and provide better service to their clients. As such, AI-powered case management systems are becoming increasingly popular in the legal industry, and we will likely see more firms adopting these technologies in the coming years.

Ultimately, determining cost-saving practices and reducing the steps required to conclude cases quicker can help law firms improve efficiency, reduce costs, and provide better client service. By automating routine tasks, using cloud-based services, reducing the number of steps, using data analytics, and continuously reviewing and improving processes, law firms can achieve these goals and remain competitive in a rapidly changing legal landscape.

CHAPTER 8:
AI AND DIFFERENT PRACTICES

Artificial Intelligence (AI) can be applied to various practices. It can revolutionize many industries and techniques, making them more efficient, effective, and sustainable. Discussed below are some of the major applications of AI and tools derived from it.

Personal injuries

Ordinary citizens are generally unaware of many legal terms, laws, and proceedings unless they encounter any adverse event in their lifetime. Personal Injuries lawsuits are associated with civil suits that individuals bring to the court of law if they experience a deliberate infliction of harm on their physical or psychological state.

The connection of AI with these types of suits to identify both simple and detailed facts and insights is getting more influential every day. The use of technology in law firms is essential to cater to cases in a more advanced way. Deploying methods and equipment capable of speeding up personal injury lawsuits more accurately has become crucial.

The list of impacts of AI in Personal Injury Practice is as follows:

- ✓ Efficient and proper intake process to achieve best lead conversion.
- ✓ Timely and calculated treatment setup and follow-up to prevent treatment gaps and maximize case value.
- ✓ Scheduling and treatments on time with a follow-up system.
- ✓ Collect all medical records.
- ✓ Collect, analyze, and calculate all medical bills.
- ✓ Analyze and estimate all injuries, current and future.
- ✓ Calculate pain and suffering based on historical data.
- ✓ Calculate and estimate lost wages.
- ✓ Prepare comprehensive demands with backup analysis.

- ✓ Deposition preparation and document collections.
- ✓ Creating a discovery list and sending out subpoenas and document requests.
- ✓ Collect, store, and analyze case materials.
- ✓ Create an offer for settlement based on information collected and historical case outcomes.
- ✓ Finally, prepare for trials, including jury selection, opening statement, and expected results. AI has access to all coaching sessions, material, and recommendations of the best litigators in this industry. Coaches and mentors that attorney travel and pay to listen to.

An AI system is connected to all that relevant content.

As per the experts, professionals in any particular field will likely need to catch up if they overlook incorporating technologically advanced machinery or procedures while solving relevant cases. Lawyers who deny the benefits of such a great innovation would need more time to stay updated and make the most of it to resolve the most complex cases. Besides, suits involving personal injuries are commonly settled down before even going into the courts by going for an option of *settlement* which is a sort of agreement between both the parties involved in a dispute to bring it to an end with the dissolution of further legal proceedings. The constitution provides this option in every democratic state to save time, money, and energy for the court and both parties.

AI tools help figure out precisely calculated compensation for the one who suffered injuries. The court of Law works on solid evidence to prove which of the two parties is guilty and which one is not. This is termed ***the burden of proof.*** During the old times, the plaintiffs often found it extremely challenging to gather all authentic and genuine evidence. Then came the technology to help provide all required to present in front of the jury. Therefore, it is simple and quick to differentiate, reach a potential conclusion, and do justice.

Employment and Labor Law Practice

An employment law practice can be quite challenging since it depends on historical information about the industry and employers. Furthermore, it also relies on state employment law and precedence. Following are some of the impacts of AI platforms on Employment Law Practice:

- ✓ The intake process usually starts with a story, unlike personal injury cases where the injury does not walk in. You start with the story and then determine the actions required.

- ✓ Asking the right questions from each client and their story is critical to identify the potential case. AI can create queries based on the story told by the client in real-time. Create follow-up questions based on answers received.
- ✓ Real-Time comparison with other past similar cases, clients, employers, and case results.
- ✓ Identify the case merits.
- ✓ Retain the client immediately if required.
- ✓ Compare the intake information to past intakes to identify the pattern to be used for Class Action Cases.
- ✓ Set up an attorney consultation with the client for further review.
- ✓ Create a list of required documents.
- ✓ Produce the document request for employment records.
- ✓ Collect, store, and analyze received documents.
- ✓ Create Pre-Lit demand letters.
- ✓ E-file the complaints.
- ✓ Identify and propose depositions to be scheduled based on past similar cases.
- ✓ Schedule deposition.

- ✓ Create deposition questions based on past successful depositions in similar cases.
- ✓ Summarize deposition recordings.
- ✓ Begin the case discovery for trial preparation.
- ✓ Assist in jury selection.
- ✓ Identify and create a summary from filed experts, mentors, and masterminds in employment law practice to create a game plan for litigation.
- ✓ Create a witness questionnaire with expected answers.
- ✓ Estimate the trial time based on historical data.
- ✓ Estimate the outcome value of the trial and the percentage of success.

Criminal cases

Evidence analysis

AI tools can help analyze large amounts of evidence, including text, audio, and video data, to identify patterns or anomalies relevant to a criminal case.

Predictive analytics

AI algorithms can analyze data from previous cases and predict the likelihood of a suspect committing a crime, the probability of a particular outcome in a case, or the potential for a suspect to re-offend.

Investigative tools

AI tools can help law enforcement agencies identify potential suspects, track criminal activity, and analyze data from various sources to identify trends or patterns.

Family law

Artificial Intelligence (AI) can transform family law by providing automated systems to assist lawyers and litigants in various tasks. Below are some ways elaborating on how AI can be used in family law:

Document automation

AI can automatically generate legal documents such as separation agreements, divorce papers, and child custody agreements. This can save time and reduce errors in drafting legal documents.

Predictive analytics

AI can analyze large amounts of data from past cases to predict the outcome of current issues. This can help lawyers and litigants to make informed decisions about their case strategy.

Case management

It can manage case files, including scheduling hearings and deadlines, tracking document submissions, and providing reminders to lawyers and litigants.

Online dispute resolution

AI facilitates online dispute resolution (ODR) by providing a neutral platform for parties to negotiate and settle disputes without going to court.

Decision-making assistance

It assists judges in making decisions by analyzing case facts, identifying relevant legal principles, and providing recommendations based on past precedents.

Immigration and the Support of AI Tools

There are various ways that AI (Artificial Intelligence) is being used in the field of immigration to ease the complex procedures of providing passengers with the best possible services:

Streamlining the application process

AI can help automate routine administrative tasks such as verifying documents, processing applications, and conducting background checks. This can reduce processing times and make the application process more efficient.

Estate planning

Estate planning and living trust are prime targets of AI legal platforms to eliminate the need for more than 70% of cases requiring legal representation.

AI platforms will eliminate the following tasks:

- ✓ Document collection.
- ✓ Financial Statement Collection and Analysis.
- ✓ Credit Reports to identify assets and liabilities.
- ✓ Real Estate information and valuation.
- ✓ Retirement accounts.
- ✓ Investment accounts.

Using the collected information combined with client objectives and demographic can help recommend the best Estate Planning Program for each client. Also, provide all the risks and prediction about the future of assets.

Attorney reviews are necessary to confirm the recommendation and calculation, but it should take a fraction of time once the AI system has done all the preparation and calculations.

IP and trademark

Intellectual property (IP) and trademarks are relevant in AI, especially with the increasing use and development of machine learning algorithms and other AI technologies. Like any other invention, AI technologies may be eligible for various forms of IP protection, such as patents, copyrights, and trade secrets. However, AI-related designs can raise unique challenges, such as determining the inventorship of an AI-generated invention or whether an AI system can be considered an author under copyright law.

AI-powered tools can be used to conduct trademark searches to identify potential conflicts with existing trademarks. These tools can also help with monitoring trademark registrations and identifying possible infringements. It can also monitor and enforce trademark rights by identifying potential infringers and counterfeiters. AI-powered brand protection tools can help companies detect and respond to system glitches.

Real estate

None of the fields of work has remained untouched by the influence of AI. It's profoundly impacting and altering how to carry out tasks proficiently. Real estate is among some sectors that took a little longer to grab the thump of meaningful changes caused by the instant developments in AI and machine learning.

Setting Property Value

AI does not hinder real estate dealers from eventually trying to steal their livelihood. Instead, it is a breakthrough in the field to uncover the latest ways of property evaluation even decades from now.

Financial Modelling

Financial modeling in real estate is the process of creating a mathematical model that represents the financial performance of a real estate investment. Financial modeling aims to project the expected returns and risks associated with the acquisition and make informed decisions based on these projections.

AI can be used in real estate financial modeling to help automate some of the processes involved in the analysis. For example, machine learning algorithms can identify patterns and trends in real estate data, which can help predict future performance.

Corporate cases

The misconception that artificial intelligence (AI) will someday supersede human control over the planet and deprive us of our livelihood seems baseless and only valid for a few decades shortly. Instead, integrating tech-based knowledge and devices in legal practices can be instrumental in revolutionizing the judiciary system's drift. In the field of corporate Law, the effects of incorporating AI tools and techniques ensure a prominent rise in productivity.

AI tools manage the drafting of lower-exposure documents such as non-disclosure agreements (NDAs); many codes and programs are designed to fetch accurate data and information from a pile of papers provided to deliberately mislead the proceedings by confusing lawyers and members of the jury. Presently, intellectuals or even common masses that are closely associated with the consumption of tech-driven gadgets, processes, and machines cannot resist the urge to accept the multi-million benefits of AI and a continual transition in the future of it.

Below are discussed some of the crucial applications of AI in the field of Law:

1. Conducting research and maintaining Credibility
2. Methods to Generate Useful Insights along with introducing an uninterrupted stream of automated processes
3. Understanding Contract Lifecycle Management (CLM)

To be precise, many experts who do not even belong to the corporate Law, including a consummate British author, Richard Susskind, have firmly believed that AI is a gateway to a flowing stream of possibilities with the absolute potential to oust archaic ways of providing justice and embracing new and more advanced practices with the most error-free ways to help the injustice victims.

We will end this chapter with the concluding remarks that it is high time lawyers and law firms adopted AI to optimize their practices and resources and face future challenges.

Conclusion

Many lawyers and law firms have to adopt AI (artificial intelligence) to optimize their practices and resources and face future challenges. By embracing AI, lawyers and law firms can save time and money and provide better client service. However, it's important to note that AI is not a replacement for human expertise and judgment and should be used to support legal professionals rather than replace them.

AI RESOURCES LIST

Law Practices

LawGeex, https://www.lawgeex.com/, Contract review automation – Their contract review automation solution is an industry-first, using patented AI technology to review and redline legal documents based on your predefined policies.

DISCO, https://csdisco.com/, DISCO brings artificial intelligence, cloud computing, and data analytics to the practice of law to let lawyers spend their time doing what matters most: securing justice for their clients and winning the most important disputes in the world.

Westlaw Edge
https://legal.thomsonreuters.com/en/products/westlaw-edge#westsearch-plus,
Westlaw Edge offers unrivaled research features powered by the most advanced AI, built on the foundation of the market-leading legal research platform.

Quick Check by Westlaw Edge

https://legal.thomsonreuters.com/en/products/westlaw-edge/quick-check

Upload a brief, and Quick Check will produce a report with recommendations for additional relevant authority, warnings for cited authority, an analysis of quotations, and a table of authorities.

Use this in-depth analysis to jumpstart your research, strengthen your arguments, pinpoint weaknesses in your opponent's positions, and compare multiple filings from a matter.

Lex Machina

https://lexmachina.com/

Lex Machina provides Legal Analytics® to companies and law firms, enabling them to craft successful litigation strategies, win cases, and close business.

ALT Legal

https://www.altlegal.com/

Alt Legal is more than great IP docketing software. You get a team invested in your success, current on all things IP, and always enhancing its software and approach. Our mission is to make life easier for trademark professionals. We accomplish this with our leading trademark docketing software and helpful community events and resources.

Logikcull

https://www.logikcull.com/

Powerful, Scalable eDiscovery Software. No more legacy tools. No more manual redaction. No more waiting around for vendors. Just connect, collect, and go. Join the Community of 1,500+ modern organizations.

ROSS

https://blog.rossintelligence.com/

ROSS Intelligence ("ROSS") builds AI-driven products to augment lawyers' cognitive abilities.

Kira

https://www.kirasystems.com/

Kira is a patented machine learning software that identifies, extracts, and analyzes content in your contracts and documents with unparalleled accuracy and efficiency. Easily find and use trusted information from your contracts and documents.

eBrevia by DFIN

https://www.dfinsolutions.com/products/ebrevia

How does eBrevia do it? By combining natural language processing technology with machine learning – a type of AI that focuses on studying algorithms. The AI-powered contract analysis software draws from a repository of thousands of legal documents to recognize language patterns and identify key concepts in documents.

Wevorce

https://www.wevorce.com/

Wevorce Private Judges are dedicated to helping couples and families get through their divorce with less stress, less emotional impact, more peace, and better preparedness for a new beginning.

Casetext

https://casetext.com/

Casetext created the first large language model trained on the law. That's one reason OpenAI chose us to use their latest model to build a product that is informed, reliable, and secure enough for professional use.

DoNotPay

https://donotpay.com/

The DoNotPay app is the home of the world's first robot lawyer. Fight corporations, beat bureaucracy, and sue anyone at the press of a button.

Luminance

https://www.luminance.com/

Luminance is the world's most advanced AI for processing legal documents, streamlining operations, and delivering value business-wide.

KLARITY

https://www.tryklarity.com/

Our vision is to eliminate the need for manual document review with best-in-class Artificial Intelligence. Current solutions involve complex workflow software that does little more than optimize handoffs between humans. The benefits are marginal at best. Klarity's deep understanding of document content, driven by one of the world's most accurate Natural Language Processing platforms, is revolutionizing document processing in the midmarket and enterprise.

TextIQ by Relativity

https://www.relativity.com/

Maximize Your Law Firm's Expertise Relativity powers 198 of the AmLaw 200. Preferred by the largest global firms, yet flexible enough for any size matter.

Genie AI

https://us.genieai.co/

Legal templates for your business, with guidance from top lawyers

AttorneyIO

https://app.attorneyio.com/

Attorney IO is a revolutionary artificial intelligence service for attorneys. It allows any attorney to input legal documents for processing by our sophisticated AI easily. The AI then outputs a selection of stunningly relevant legal cases.

Fast Data Science

https://fastdatascience.com/

Extracting Value from Unstructured Data. Text, Natural Language Processing, Machine Learning, Healthcare, Pharma, Legal, and Insurance, towards a healthy world with the help of AI

iManage

https://imanage.com/solutions/law-firms/

Law firms run on knowledge. The iManage knowledge work platform empowers law firms to work intelligently and securely, unlocking productivity and expertise to drive better results for you and your clients. Our platform enables various integrated solutions to help law firms manage knowledge more effectively while mitigating risk, improving compliance, and ensuring security and governance.

Harvey by Allen & Overy

https://www.allenovery.com/

Allen & Overy (A&O), the leading international law firm, has broken new ground by integrating Harvey, the innovative artificial intelligence platform built on a version of Open AI's latest models enhanced for legal work, into its global practice. Harvey will empower more than 3,500 A&O lawyers across 43 offices operating in multiple languages with the ability to generate and access legal content with unmatched efficiency, quality, and intelligence.

Advanced

https://www.oneadvanced.com/solutions/legal/

Trusted by more than 5,000 law firms and barristers' chambers and with over 30 years of experience. Work smarter, communicate more effectively, and deliver legal services quickly and securely through our trusted legal solutions. Our end-to-end legal-centric software provides you with the accuracy and flexibility to identify opportunities for growth and greater efficiency while working in a secure environment wherever your team works from.

rradar

https://www.rradar.com/

We are a specialist litigation and commercial law firm that uses legal expertise and digital tools to proactively manage, advise and deliver business solutions to reduce legal risk.

NALANDA

https://nalandatechnology.com/

Nalanda was founded with the vision to develop and deliver innovative, intuitive, and efficient core software solutions. Our focus is on helping anyone who is at a loss in navigating and managing their electronic documents and data.

CARA AI

https://casetext.com/cara-info

How does CARA A.I. find on-point cases so quickly? CARA A.I. uses artificial intelligence technology developed by Casetext to find cases and other authorities on the same facts and legal issues in the documents you upload. CARA A.I. can help you find a relevant precedent even if you only upload a one-page motion draft. The more information you give CARA A.I., its recommendations will be more accurate.

ATLAS by Workland

https://www.workland.com/atlas/

The extensive use of AI tools in recruitment is still somewhat controversial, as critics worry software will "learn" or inherit human bias and inadvertently systematize discrimination. However, many law firms use AI tools for simple tasks like scheduling interviews, making travel arrangements, sending targeted job listings, and screening thousands of resumes for the best candidates.

PCLaw | Time Matters

https://pclawtimematters.com/

PCLaw | Time Matters™ offers practice management solutions tens of thousands of users use worldwide. We help legal professionals enhance their productivity and profitability, allowing them to help more people worldwide.

LexCheck

https://www.lexcheck.com/

Improve your legal team's performance and culture with instant redlines on incoming contracts.

Everlaw

https://www.everlaw.com/

Everlaw is a cloud-based e-discovery platform that unlocks the collaborative power of litigation and investigative teams.

hyperlex by DiliTrust

https://hyperlex.ai/en/

DiliTrust is a unified suite of 5 modules to digitize and automate all your company's legal activities and gain productivity. Thanks to it, you can share and collaborate in complete security, anywhere, anytime. On the DiliTrust media site, discover articles, videos, and content to download that will help you digitize your practices.

Evisort

https://www.evisort.com/

AI has always been core to Evisort, founded out of Harvard and MIT in 2016 when three law and data science students discovered the immense potential of AI-powered contract intelligence at scale.

blue J

https://www.bluej.com/

At Blue J, we leverage the power of artificial intelligence and industry-leading legal expertise to help you to deliver the answers and insight you need to be successful. Our platform is designed to improve productivity while enabling your team to focus on higher-value tasks.

WiseTime

https://wisetime.com/

At WiseTime, we were recently granted a patent in the US for our unique timeline algorithm. Our innovative software also uses AI to help law firms improve their internal processes, and it's the first of its kind in the legal sector.

LegalZoom

https://www.legalzoom.com/

We're for technology that makes it easy, attorneys and tax experts who make it seem effortless, and trusted partners who make the next hurdle feel like less of a leap.

ClearLaw

https://www.clearlaw.ai/

Clearlaw's proprietary Nature Language Processing (NLP) engine was built by Stanford PhDs and JDs who had grown frustrated with the repetitive processes and lack of data while reviewing in-house corporate contracts. Thinking there must be a better way, they created a robust AI platform that empowers attorneys, paralegals, and legal operations teams by connecting them to existing technology and processes.

Notion AI

https://www.notion.so/product/ai

Access the limitless power of AI right inside Notion. Work faster. Write better. Think bigger.

LEXOO

https://info.lexoo.com/

We think legal work can be easier. Finding better ways to use technology, process, and talent means we can unlock capacity and efficiency and improve stakeholders' feelings when they receive legal advice.

Notarize

https://www.notarize.com/

Notarize is the leader in online notarization, which is simpler, smarter, and safer than notarizing documents on paper. Notarize brings trust online 24/7 for life's most important moments, from buying or selling a home to adopting a child.

Legal Robot

https://legalrobot.com/

We use several types of machine learning, including a technique called Deep Learning, to construct abstract representations of the language in a legal document. These abstractions allow us to look at the topics across a large set of legal documents and use statistical techniques to identify potential issues in your document.

Leverton

https://mricontractintelligence.com/

The power behind Contract Intelligence adopts an AI-first mentality into your business for fast data extraction, analysis, and insight to unlock your contracts' value.

ContractPodAi

https://contractpodai.com/

With ContractPodAi Cloud, we're extending the same power and utility — that we brought to contracting — to the entire legal lifecycle of your business. Now, you and your team can leverage One Legal Platform to handle any use case and face any work challenge. And our commitment to a phased implementation — combined with our legal and software expertise — ensures a seamless legal digital transformation.

ThoughtRiver

https://www.thoughtriver.com/

Legal professionals across the globe spend countless hours grinding their way through contract reviews. Our Contract Acceleration Platform is changing that for the better with sophisticated AI. We help lawyers to deliver more business value and achieve greater job satisfaction by freeing up their time for higher-level strategic work.

CaseMine

https://www.casemine.com/

At CaseMine, we believe that the only thing constant is change itself. Hence, we have continuously and tirelessly sought ways to innovate legal research. Harnessing the power of Artificial Intelligence, our unique document analysis system captures the essence of your legal research. CaseIQ, our AI-enabled research tool, extracts the facto - legal matrix of any document uploaded onto it. As a result, the retrieved authorities are clinching precedents - as they mirror the context of the document uploaded on to CaseIQ.

Intraspexion

https://intraspexion.com/

Intraspexion is a Sequim, Washington-based company that uses deep learning algorithms to alert corporate legal teams regarding risks of internal litigation in near real-time. It essentially provides an early warning system for legal issues. In 2018, Intraspexion's deep learning patent portfolio grew to eight, more than anyone's except Google, IBM, Microsoft, and Siemens Healthcare.

PracticeLeague ELM Platform

https://www.practiceleague.com/

PracticeLeague is an enterprise that deals in advanced legal technology. Over 8,000 lawyers have revolutionized their workflow models using their solutions. PRACTICELEAGUE Legal AI Software uses SaaS-based products that automate clients' legal practices and is deployed in several law firms and legal departments across the globe. The company provides an intelligent technology grid for the entire legal ecosystem and an integrated and intelligent enterprise management platform that boosts legal efficiency and cost-effectiveness.

LegalSifter

https://www.legalsifter.com/

LegalSifter builds simple, affordable AI solutions that help users manage their legal obligations and opportunities. It uses natural language processing and machine learning to turn unstructured terms, conditions, and words into structured data and insights.

Neota

https://www.neotalogic.com/

Neota Logic is the developer of an AI platform for the legal and compliance space. Its drag-and-drop solution allows enterprises to automate processes and combine reasoning, judgments, rules, and document automation to overcome legal challenges.

LawPavilion

https://www.lawpavilion.com/

LawPavilion is a digital research and practice management solution for the legal space. Developed by Grace InfoTech Limited, its portfolio contains cutting-edge solutions for legal practitioners, judges, and academicians. LawPavilion is a useful tool for quick legal research and has improved how the law is practiced in Africa.

Gauge Data Solutions

http://www.gaugeanalytics.com/

Using AI, Gauge underlines linkages between case laws that are not immediately apparent, thereby enabling in-depth and comprehensive legal research. Its solutions enable researchers to move beyond keyword-based searches—in law- and searches are often constrained by the number of keywords the associate assigned to a legal proposition knows.

Brightflag

https://brightflag.com/

The shine platform eliminates many of the problems of old e-billing systems - no costly implementation, no change management programs with outside law firms, and providing accurate spend analysis aimed at getting the maximum value from outside counsel spending. It reduces costs on outside spending, saves time processing invoices, and helps improve relationships with outside counsel.

Marketing

Jasper, https://www.jasper.ai/, Jasper is an exceptional AI content generator with more than 52 short and long-form writing templates. Whether you're writing a personal bio, an Instagram photo caption, an Amazon product description, or a real estate listing, Jasper can fix you with content designed (and proven to) convert.

Copysmith, https://copysmith.ai/, Copysmith is designed to help brands and businesses reach their content goals. Copysmith's AI content generator makes product description writing fast, easy, and fun – are you ready for your mind to be blown?

Kafkai, https://kafkai.com/, Kafkai is the oldest AI content generator geared specifically toward creating SEO-relevant content. The software works with a niche writing system, unlike typical templates. It offers article writing in 37 niches, including health, sports, dogs, SEO, and software.

Article Forge, https://www.articleforge.com/, This AI writing tool creates original SEO content using deep learning in less than a minute. Feed Article Forge your keyword and any other relevant information, and it will create an article complete with relevant subheadings, AI-generated images, videos, and links.

Articoolo, http://articoolo.com/, Articoolo works on an article purchase basis; readers pay to generate a fixed number of articles per month or plan. After entering the keyword, the software generates a short article, typically under 500 words.

Rytr, https://rytr.me/, Rytr is a straightforward writing assistant and content generator with over 30 templates and use cases. It is aimed at helping copywriters, and content marketers generate copy for ads, landing pages, product descriptions, and more.

CopyAI, https://www.copy.ai/, CopyAI is another popular artificial intelligence writing software. With over 90 tools for content writing and copywriting, it's no wonder the tool has over 1 million users.

Peppertype, https://www.peppertype.ai/. Peppertype was created by one of the world's largest content marketplaces—Pepper Content. Using GPT-3, this AI writing assistant helps with content idea generation and content and copy.

Marketmuse, https://www.marketmuse.com/, Marketmuse is an AI tool for content planning and optimization. Marketers use it to analyze millions of articles in real-time. This helps uncover knowledge gaps and opportunities to create better content than the existing ones in a given industry.

Sparktoro, https://sparktoro.com/, Sparktoro is an audience intelligence platform for uncovering deep and accurate insights about an audience. For example, it shows what websites an audience reads, and which influences they follow.

BuzzSumo, https://buzzsumo.com/, BuzzSumo is an AI content marketing tool for content research and engagement analysis.

Otter AI, https://otter.ai/, Otter AI is an AI tool for transcribing recorded meetings to notes. It can transcribe your online meeting in real-time and store it in a central place for easy search and use.

WriteSonic, https://writesonic.com/, Writesonic is built on GPT-3 and claims the machine is trained on the content that the brands using the tool produce. The generator is based on facilitating marketing copy, blog articles, and product descriptions. The generator can also provide content ideas and outlines and has a full suite of templates for different types of content.

Frase, https://www.frase.io/, Frase is a content assistant targeted to content marketers and SEO professionals for faster and better productivity. The tool is structured around a framework of content brief, content writing, content optimization, and content analytics.

AI Writer, https://ai-writer.com/, AI Writer pitches itself as SEO-friendly, producing fresh and relevant copy that can save you 50% of your writing time.

Hyperwrite, https://hyperwriteai.com/, Hyperwrite claims to use the most advanced AI generator. It's one of the most basic tools to use and generate content and the only fully free tool.

INK, INK is another AI-powered tool targeted at content marketers and SEO experts as a content assistant for faster output and optimized content.

Snazzy (Now Smart Copy by Unbounce), https://snazzy.ai/, Snazzy is powered by GPT-3 and their proprietary machine learning to create a tool focused on landing page generation.

Long Shot, https://www.longshot.ai/, Long shot pitches itself as an AI-powered long-form content assistant to produce SEO-friendly content built on a combination of GPT-3 and custom AI models.

Scalenut, https://www.scalenut.com/, If you're a website owner or SEO manager looking to rank higher on Google, Scalenut is a great option. Using Scalenut's SEO features, you can optimize your articles for maximum visibility in search engines. Scalenut's AI technology can analyze your existing content and provide briefs and topic suggestions. It can also find related SEO-friendly keywords and topics to improve your website's ranking on search engines.

ContentBot AI, https://contentbot.ai/, Contentbot.ai is a versatile tool designed for founders, copywriters, digital marketers, bloggers, and SEO Specialists. With Contentbot, you can easily create top-notch content for blog posts, advertisements, and landing pages.

QuillBot, https://quillbot.com/, QuillBot is a free AI writer and paraphrasing tool that allows you to rewrite the content or generate a new one with just a few clicks. It contains many features, such as a grammar checker, paraphrasing tool, co-writing, plagiarism checker, and summarizer tool.

Simplified AI, https://simplified.com/ai-writer/, Simplified AI is much more than just an AI Copywriting Generator — it also offers graphic design tools, a video editor, animation tools, social media scheduling, and more. This makes it the perfect all-in-one solution for your content needs.

Smodin, https://smodin.io/, Smodin is a free AI text generator that helps users create unique and plagiarism-free articles and essays.

With Smodin, provide a prompt with a few words, and the tool will generate content in a fraction of the time. Smodin can help you generate different types of content, such as articles, essays, blog posts, and more.

Shortly AI, https://www.shortlyai.com/, Shortly AI is one of the first artificial intelligence writing tools that Uses the power of GPT-3 technology from OpenAI, now owned by Jasper. Shortly AI was created to assist those who are having difficulty creating content.

Content Generation

Wordtune, https://www.wordtune.com/, Wordtune is an AI writing software built to understand your text and make suggestions on how to make it clearer.

Anyword, https://anyword.com/, Anyword has many copywriting frameworks, making it an ideal tool for creating a conversion-driven copy.

GrowthBar, https://www.growthbarseo.com/, If you're on the lookout for an AI solution that can give you a hand with your SEO, then Growthbar could be a top-notch choice for you! With Growtbar, you can access many SEO tools to help your content rank on search engines.

Creaitor.ai, https://www.creaitor.ai/, Save hours on writing content and get out of the idea jam Creaitor has taken marketing to a completely different level. With its good AD copies, Creaitor has given new perspectives, leading to measurable success in acquiring new customers.

Article Forge, https://www.articleforge.com/, Article Forge differs from the previous marketing tools in that it allows AI to generate the content for you instead of just allowing you to optimize the content you've written. It's one of the leading content generator tools because it generates entire articles for you.

Ink for All, https://inkforall.com/?fpr=rachel71, Ink for All is AI writing software that facilitates putting your ideas into ones that also resonate with others. Ink for All allows you to write content within the app and add it as a browser extension to get all the features.

Closers Copy, https://www.closerscopy.com/?ref=aaxt, Closers Copy is an AI writing software that is great for marketing copy. Their website claims that other AI writing generators don't provide the type of software ideal for generating marketing copy.

Grammarly, https://www.grammarly.com/, Grammarly is an AI-powered writing app extension for proofreading and editing your content in real time. It detects writing errors in grammar, lexis and structure, and punctuation. It also suggests corrections for every mistake it detects. Let's highlight some of Grammarly's core features.

Persado, https://www.persado.com/, Persado provides the only Motivation AI platform that enables personalized communications at scale, inspiring each individual to engage and act.

Adobe Target, https://business.adobe.com/, Adobe Target uses AI to create personalized content experiences for users based on their behavior and interests.

BlueConic, https://www.blueconic.com/, BlueConic is an enterprise tool that uses machine learning to analyze customer data and create personalized user experiences based on their preferences and interests.

Surfer, https://surferseo.com/, Surfer is an AI-powered content creation tool that combines keyword research, content editing, domain analysis, and SERP analysis with content planning to ensure you're always writing relevant content. There are a lot of features that this tool has when it comes to all things content writing.

Outranking, https://www.outranking.io/, Outranking is an AI content strategy platform that doesn't stop content creation. It tracks previous content performance and helps you with content planning and strategy – making a seamless experience from start to finish.

Narrato Workspace, https://narrato.io/, Narrato Workspace is an AI-powered content planning, creation, and collaboration platform that lets you manage all your content operations in one place. Narrato's powerful AI capabilities include an intuitive AI writing assistant, an AI content assistant for quality optimization, an SEO content brief generator for search optimization and research, an AI topic generator, and AI images. Narrato eliminates the need for multiple tools in the content process and replaces a scattered, disjointed tool stack with a single, user-friendly platform.

WriteMe.Ai, https://writeme.ai/, WriteMe.Ai is an up-and-coming writing tool for anyone looking to boost their productivity and creativity. Its powerful features such as chat with AI, SEO writing, and multilingual content, simplify the writing process and help you create high-quality content in no time. Whether you're a blogger, writer, marketer, or creative, WriteMe.Ai has everything you need to take your writing to the next level.

Neural Text, https://www.neuraltext.com/, Neural Text is another platform that allows you to get AI-generated content based on keywords you input. Many niches and fields utilize this type of writing. Business and healthcare are two examples.

Case Study

Trinka, https://www.trinka.ai/, Trinka is an AI-powered writing assistant created with academic writing in mind. It'll spot technical and scientific writing errors that other common grammar and spelling tools may miss. So, whether you're working on a paper in medicine or economics, Trinka can recommend improvements relevant to your subject. Trinka will also identify and correct your vocabulary, grammar, spelling, syntax use, tone, and more. It can even make suggestions to make your academic paper more compliant with the APA or AMA style guides.

ProofHub, https://www.proofhub.com/, ProofHub is packed with all the features your teams need to plan, collaborate, organize, and deliver projects on time. It helps your teams work together in the easiest, fastest and smartest way with all the right tools under one roof.

ResearchGate, https://www.researchgate.net/, ResearchGate gives you access to over 135 million publication pages, allowing you to stay updated with what's happening in your field.

Wizdom.ai, https://www.wizdom.ai/, Wizdom.ai is an AI-powered software that provides insights to make the right and impactful decisions. It provides wisdom with its powerful artificial intelligence system that can monitor, analyze, and interpret billions of data points. In this way, this platform provides actionable insights for decision-making to everyone, including governments, institutions, researchers, and funders.

Semantic Scholar, https://www.semanticscholar.org/, is the finest AI software for researchers, developed by the Allen Institute for Artificial Intelligence, and is a free tool for scholarly journals. They aim to help researchers avoid information overload by making the best of what's available in the world's scientific literature more accessible.

Leverton, https://mricontractintelligence.com/, The power behind Contract Intelligence Adopt an AI-first mentality into your business for fast data extraction, analysis, and insight so you can unlock the value of your contracts.

Notion AI, https://www.notion.so/product/ai, Access the limitless power of AI right inside Notion. Work faster. Write better. Think bigger.

KLARITY, https://www.tryklarity.com/, Our vision is to eliminate the need for manual document review with best-in-class Artificial Intelligence. Current solutions involve complex workflow software that does little more than optimize handoffs between humans. The benefits are marginal at best. Klarity's deep understanding of document content, driven by one of the world's most accurate Natural Language Processing platforms, is revolutionizing document processing in the midmarket and enterprise.

Logikcull, https://www.logikcull.com/, Powerful, Scalable eDiscovery Software. No more legacy tools. No more manual redaction. No more waiting around for vendors. Just connect, collect, and go. Join the Community of 1,500+ modern organizations.

ABOUT AUTHOR

Hamid Kohan is a force to be reckoned with in technology and innovation. A veritable Silicon Valley veteran, Kohan has consistently proven himself as a trailblazer, turning bold ideas into tangible realities that have left an indelible mark on the industry. Throughout his illustrious career, he has held several leadership roles, including a successful tenure as the president of a publicly traded company. His wealth of experience and relentless pursuit of innovation have led him to his current role as a pioneering tech entrepreneur, focusing on revolutionizing the medical and legal industries.

Driven to make a tangible difference in the world, Kohan has founded multiple companies within the legal and medical sectors, including Legal Soft, a law firm growth company currently serving over 650 law firms, helping firms scale and expand through innovative marketing and staffing services. His unyielding passion for innovation has led him to explore the myriad possibilities offered by artificial intelligence

(AI), which he believes holds the key to transforming these industries. With his extensive leadership experience and keen understanding of technology's potential, Kohan is set to usher in a new era of progress in both fields.

Additionally, Kohan founded Lien Networks, a tech company focused on bridging the gap between lawyers and doctors working on liens, allowing them to refer cases and manage the client journey through an innovative platform. Aside from Kohan's involvement in the tech space, he is also the foundation of his own law firm, Magic Law Group. Magic Law Group is a premiere nationwide law firm that serves clients from all 50 states, specializing in personal injury, lemon law, employment, and immigration practice areas.

One of Kohan's core beliefs is that AI can bridge the gap between the wealth of information available and the speed at which professionals in the medical and legal fields must make critical decisions. By applying advanced machine learning techniques and developing intelligent algorithms, his companies are already making strides in diagnosing complex medical conditions, expediting legal research, and uncovering insights that would otherwise remain hidden within vast data sets.

Not one to rest on his laurels, Kohan also serves as an active mentor and advisor to a new generation of entrepreneurs, sharing his knowledge, experience, and passion for innovation. He firmly believes in the power of collaboration and the importance of fostering a supportive ecosystem to nurture the next wave of groundbreaking ideas. As he continues to break new ground and challenge the status quo, there is no doubt that his work will have a lasting impact on the world around us, improving the lives of millions. With his unparalleled vision and relentless drive for innovation, Hamid Kohan inspires all those who aspire to make a difference through the power of technology.